THE TIME IS NOW

For Peace On Earth

THE TEACHERS
With

Lauren C. Granger

AirPropel Books

AIRPROPEL

THE TIME IS NOW
LAUREN C. GRANGER
Copyright 2018 by Lauren C Granger
For reproduction permission, contact publisher:
AirPropel Books

LaurenCGranger.com, lauren@laurenCgranger.com
Printed in the United States of America
First Printing, 2017

ISBN: 0998178411
ISBN 9780998178417
LIBRARY OF CONGRESS
Library of Congress Control Number: 2017907647

TABLE OF CONTENTS

A MESSAGE FROM LAUREN

THE TIME IS NOW is the second book presented by the teachers. I have heard that there will be three books in this series. The Time Is Now continues with the theme of peace on earth, with more clarity, guidance, and a call for action.

As I said before, I believe everyone has the ability to hear or see in the spiritual realm. To be clear, the Teachers in this book (and the other books) are in spiritual form. I'm in physical form. The teachers talk to me and I convert their words or images into written words. What I do is not weird or special. It's just that, more than some people, I've developed the ability. I was aware of occasionally seeing and hearing without eyes and ears for most of my life. It was no big deal and I didn't make anything of it. Actually I assumed everyone did the same.

In adulthood, while a student of clinical psychology, I learned about journaling and later encouraged many of my clients to journal. It was through conversing in journals that I became aware of the teachers, and their request to present knowledge through books to share with the world. Over time, it became easier to sit with a keyboard and type as they spoke.

The ability to converse is easier with awareness. Especially when my brain is "zoned out" such as when I'm doing simple, repetitive, non-thinking tasks like washing dishes, sweeping the floor or day dreaming while on the tread mill. Stuff I could do without using brain concentration. It's as if a portal opens when the brain concentration diminishes. It's automatic and does not require assistance. I would bet that everyone does this but just doesn't recognize it.

My invisible friends (not just the teachers) are very special to me. I suspect that I talk to them more than to people in physical form. After all, they are non-judgmental, always available, knowledgeable, loving, and often funny. The perfect friends. You all have wonderful invisible friends. I don't think its weird- just something you might want to get used to.

PART ONE

THE TIME IS NOW - FOR PEACE ON EARTH

Welcome to an understanding of the spiritual-physical connection; a way to live more fully and lovingly with more ease. You see, you were never meant to be self-sufficient with only a brain, emotions, and a body. Many of you probably noticed that a large part of the puzzle, the equation, was missing. The missing piece is an overview of it all- the reason, the how to, the understanding and acceptance. Your spirit holds this part of you. The good news is that your spirit is a part of you. The answers are not in a mysterious "something" in the great unknown, the unknown that you won't find until you are dead. The only rules to follow will come from within. No one will be making up different sets of rules and demanding that you obey. The rules are infinite, unchanging, and available to all.

Now, the search for this spirit within will begin.

Let's start with saying that it is good, and should be comforting to know that you are complete. Let me add that love is a part of your make-up... infinite love. You are wired and attached to the greatest power that exists. We suggest that in times of need, you tune in instead of out- of this great power within. Your choice, as always.

YOUR BEGINNINGS

We want to say more about the beginning. The beginning of time, the beginning of loving yourself. The beginning of you before you had a brain or a body. All of you are magnificent. Before being in body, you were peaceful. You were accepting of all others- without judgment. One way of saying this is that you were pure of heart. Pure in kindness. For the most part, you left your earthly problems behind when you entered the non-physical realm. Oh, there were a few exceptions with some who were lost and confused for a while. But it didn't take long for those few to find their loving self. They had much support from others in the spiritual realm who wanted nothing more than to offer loving support to the new arrival... no matter the circumstances leading up to the transition.

This is important to know. We think it is good for you to know that there is and was a time of peace, love, and acceptance for each of you. That you all experienced this and still could understand, witness, and feel the feelings of people on Earth.

We feel that it is also important for you to know that you- each and every one of you will return to a place of peace. You will be welcomed back and you will, in turn, welcome others when they return.

MEANWHILE

Meanwhile, here you are, in between, in physical form, having all kinds of experiences while creating a movement of energy. Deep within is that peaceful part of you. The part which doesn't judge.The part that lives from love, not fear. Remember, fear is the part that creates all kinds of negative emotions such as anger, hate, jealousy, depression.... Fear is the emotion that separates you from your true self, your beginning self; yourself which "you" began as your loving self. That part is still with you. Maybe it got buried under all the physical adventurous emotions that you experience. Maybe the other stuff began to separate you from your beginning. Maybe you didn't know about your spirit self. Maybe the brain wasn't developed and able to tell you about your deeper loving self. It wasn't. It couldn't. We are telling you. We are your guides. We are your people who love you unconditionally. The ones who accept you no matter your experiences. Even in physical form where dark and light, long and short energy exists, you are loved in the midst of it all. At any time, you can tune in to your own "love within" and reconnect with your true self. We, your guides are always here to help you. That is what you need to know for now. Know this, beyond all else. Believe this. Believe that you are love, you are loved, and guides are here to help you.

ALL IS FAIR
Now, moving on, we will tell you that all is fair. All is fair in a wondrous way. We mean to say that each and every one of you is equal to the other. Don't overlook this important information. The base of every single person is love. Every one of you is life and all life is love. It can be no other way. That is your base, your connection to the whole. Everyone has it. Am I making myself clear? Do you understand that the really bad person has a base in love? The really bad person is acting on physical conditions and beliefs which created negative behavior. Negative behavior or as we say, negative energy, exists. We want to eradicate negative energy on Earth. It is possible. It can be done. It will be done. The point we want to make is that everyone must look deeper to find the good, the love. Everyone must look deeper to find their own loving connection. This will eliminate judgments and all the problems judgment causes.

AN EXPERIMENT IN LOOKING DEEPER. SEEING PAST YOUR CURRENT VIEW
We want to teach you how to do this. To be clear, the answer is not "out there." Out there people both physical and non-physical, can guide and make suggestions but only YOU can willingly journey to your inner depth of truth. Really, it's a fun journey of discovery. And the rewards are shall we say, out of this world. It may take years to go through all the layers of beliefs that you now have. No problem. You have time. You have an eternity to connect with your inner loving

self. We suggest that you begin by questioning your beliefs. What do you believe, where did the belief come from, how long can you remember having it. How has it helped or hindered you? You get the idea. Any subject will do for starters. All paths always go to the same answer.

Religion is always a big belief. Where did yours come from, how long have you had it, has it helped or hindered you? Often it came from your family, which came from their community, which is a part of their government…. If you challenge the religion, you may suffer a loss. Suffering creates conformity. Keep going, you haven't made it to your inner self. You will probably pass through layers of self-worth for accepting or challenging the religious belief instilled in you. This could take months or years to get through. Keep going. Once you find that you are OK and reconstruct your beliefs of self-worth, you will probably start feeling a release. Keep going layer after layer until there is nothing left but love for yourself and others.

You can do this same experiment with any subject, large or small. Start by thinking about it. Question it. Then move on to the feelings that will circulate through you. Stay until you get to love. In the beginning, this may take a lifetime. After practice, the process gets easier and faster. Start somewhere. Finish with love and acceptance for you and all of life.

WE ARE ALL ONE THROUGH OUR CONNECTION TO THE WHOLE

There is much to say. We will take time and go into depth on how to connect and live from your inner self. We are all one. When all the leaves connect to the branch, and the branch connects to the trunk, and the trunk connects to the roots, the root to the seed, there is oneness. You are all connected to each other through the energy of oneness. Your physical form may change through the seasons of your physical existence, but your energy remains a constant. Your soul, your spirit, whatever you call it… your energy within connects you to the whole- to all. Know this. Get to know this as well as you know your name. Get to know this and feel your connection. Feel the joy and the love knowing this is a truth. It can be no other way.

BE KIND TO YOURSELF AND OTHERS

The Time Is Now - For Peace on Earth. Welcome to an understanding of the spiritual-physical connection, a way to live more fully and lovingly with more ease. You see, you were never meant to be self-sufficient with only a brain, emotions, and a body. Many of you probably noticed that a large part of the puzzle, the equation, was missing. The missing piece is an overview of it all- the reason, the how to, the understanding and acceptance. Your spirit holds this part of you. The good news is that your spirit is a part of you. The answers are not in a mysterious "something" in the great unknown; the unknown you won't find until you are dead. The only rules to follow will come from within. No one will be making up different sets of rules and demanding that you obey. The rules are infinite, unchanging, and available to all.

PEACE TREATIES

Now it is time to experience- to learn about peace treaties, getting the big bang in time. A peace treaty is really nothing more or less than an agreement of kindness and respect towards each other. Create treaties of peace regularly... daily, with all your interactions. You might find it to be amazing the number of times you can send and receive genuine smiles during a conversation. Peace treaties. Agreements of acceptance.

We are very convinced, we are proud to say, that peace will reign on Earth. Each person will play a part. Each person will begin to see the advantage of getting along. Now is the time. A good time for peace treaties.

UNDERSTANDING THE MEANING OF COMPASSION

Do you understand the meaning of compassion? Do you understand that inside of you, there is a part, an energy that cares about the continuation of life? Compassion is the continuation of life, the continuation of a physical mass. The physical mass moves energy. The goal is to move powerful high frequency energy. All physical forms had the purpose of moving this energy when they chose to re-enter on this physical planet. We suggest compassion for times when people stray from the path. Keep in mind that their brain did not know any more than your brain knew, the spiritual purpose of entering the physical. Look at what you are doing. Are your actions driving others further from the path of positive energy? Does your correctional system reinforce negative energy? Change it. Recreate the wheel. Get on the path with compassion and understanding.

THE TIME IS NOW

Let's write about the time being now. It is exciting for us to see a new world coming, magnificent to see a rise in positive energy. Yes, attention has come to the violence on Earth, brought on by shining the light on the abundance of negative energy. We assure you, a wake-up call was necessary- a sharp, clear wake-up call. No more hiding the negative energy, the violence, hatred etc., in darkness, secluded places, or behind walls. The energy both negative and positive cannot be contained. It has no limit.

However, energy can be directed. We want you all to know that the key is to tune into the positive energy of love, joy, happiness, and all of its wonderful components. Negative energy will go dormant if not used. For that matter, so will positive energy. Want to fix a problem, choose your energy. Promote a better Earth or promote devastation. Your choice. Let me tell you- start now. Start now by saying something kind. View the world through eyes of kindness, then speak of it. Now is the time for kindness.

We will continue to talk of now. NOW. We are absolutely sure that NOW is the time for change. The river is beginning to flow in a new direction. NOW. Everyone is important to this movement, this flow. Know it or not, each of you contributes in one way or another. Everyone. No exceptions. You will feel the movement in your spirit, and in your physical form. We celebrate you for being on Earth at this chosen time. We are asking you to become aware of your beliefs, thoughts, behaviors. Doing so creates enlightenment. Who are you, what is your position? Come to know YOU on a deeper level. Talk about your continuation of life on Earth. Talk about peace. With love, we ask this of you. It is with love that we speak. Love, the highest frequency, longest reaching, purest, brightest energy. Let it be... here on Earth.

NOW IS A FINE TIME FOR PEACE

It's a fine time. Consider the finest. Consider a time of peace for everyone. A time of peace inside the spirit of everyone on Earth. In time, no one will be told to be kind. No one will be leery of peace. No one will be peaceful yet looking for non-peace. Consider that the time has come towards the direction of peace. The one and only way to accomplish this is by changing your thoughts, behaviors, and actions into peacefulness. YOU. The only thing keeping you from this peace is a desire from within. If you are looking for blame or judgment, then you are not looking for peace. If you are looking to carry on the momentum of anger or judgment you are not looking at peace. You can't be a winner until you stop the game. Stop the game by not playing. There are millions of people who have stopped playing. Join them. Celebrate peace with them. Become one of the believers of peace. It is now time for a fine world... a peaceful world. We are telling you that it's your time for greatness. Rejoice.

LOVE YOUR ENEMY

This isn't the first time for you to hear about loving kindness towards those you don't like. Do you NOW understand the power within? Do you understand that only loving kindness can win the game of life on Earth? Do you understand that anger, hate, etc., no matter who started it, can only continue the cycle? Can you see that loving kindness will stop the battle no matter who starts it? We want you to know, to practice kindness towards those people you don't like. Don't respond in kind to the person who hurt you, who murdered someone special to you but stop the violence, change the game. Love is the only answer.

We get it. We understand that love will not be immediate. Do you understand that hating back will continue the game? Do you get that being on the level of understanding, healing, accepting, loving will change the game? Learning to love is the only hope for the victim, the perpetrator, the world. Not the physical love connection to each other. You are all connected to the power, the energy of infinite love. Reflecting it towards your enemy is a good use of that energy. Your infinite connection to the whole, to god, the source of all is your answer.

A CELEBRATION OF JOY DAY

It is good news day, a day of celebration. We invite every one of you to celebrate life today. No matter what your day is about, you all have the ability to celebrate life. To celebrate, be happy. Be consciously aware of happiness. It is that simple. Everyone, choose an energy for today. Choose joy. Choose to allow the infinite love within. Choose to accept a path of joy today. Let's name it JOY DAY. Now that is worth celebrating! This will be easy to do if life is going your way. If you've got more money, more love, more stuff, then this will be an easy Joy Day of celebration. You may think this is difficult if life were difficult today. If a loved one died, a trauma occurred, your money is gone, and so are your home and/or loved ones. The rules are the same. What applies to one day applies to another. Joy is in abundance for everyone. With or without circumstances, celebrate joy today.

Today, celebrate what you had, have, will have, and what is eternally yours. You see. We aren't asking for you to celebrate the situations of today. We are asking you to celebrate your purpose in life. Celebrate your full range of experiences for the purpose of joy, the purpose of transmitting positive energy throughout forever. Can you do that? Can you find moments of joy to celebrate today? Moments of gratefulness. We think you can. Join Joy Day on planet Earth today. Invite someone to celebrate with you.

THE WAR ON PEACE

Do you see the conflict within that statement? Peace is a topic of interest for most people-- personal peace, relationship peace, community, or world peace, no matter which side of the discussion, or belief you are on. Many people believe so strongly in their own position that they are willing to fight over it, kill over it. We see that as non-peace. If peace has to be fought over, then peace isn't being created. For all your battles, lay down your fear. Put your fear down and come out with a smile, a handshake, an embrace. To lay down your fear means your weapons of power. In the end, those weapons are worthless in the battle for peace. We ask both sides to become vulnerable to peace, to love, to a connection. Take the risk. Open your heart instead of your trigger. The power is within. Both love and fear are from within.

Consider how intimidating you look to the person facing your gun. It is not the look of love which you have created with that gun. It is another fear, another violence, another intimidation, another energy that planet Earth doesn't need. Stop creating fear!

Both sides are creating. At the end of your day, will you say "I created love" or will you say "I created fear and intimidation." Each of you, on an individual basis must make the choice. Your boss, your community, your leader, can't make the choice for you. Make it personal. Create that which you truly desire.

I just heard someone say, "I desire to blow that person away." We say fear is what you are expressing. A fear disguised as power. You have the power to heal. A fear of separation, a fear of tolerance, a fear of lack. Whether or not you recognize it, your desire is based in fear not in power, not in strength. Perhaps you aren't afraid to "blow that person away." Perhaps you are afraid of you, afraid of experiencing the love within. Do you know what it feels like—the love, connection?

What we want to tell you is that blowing someone away does not expand positive energy. It will not cure any part of you or the world. Blowing someone away creates shorter wavelength, negative energy. More of what you are experiencing. It is the negative energy that separates you from the other person. It is negative energy that separates you from your peace. We are saying that you are love. You are loved. Connect to the infinite love within you. That other person is also loved. Connect with that other person from a place of infinite love and acceptance. That is where you will find strength. That is where your power is held. Your power is in your love, so lay down your fear. Learn the difference.

BECOMING ONE WITH SELF IS BECOMING ONE WITH GOD
Your shortest journey in physical distance will be to the depth of your love within. Your longest journey through time will be to your love within. If you haven't already, now is a good time to start.

Your love within is a part of your make up—a part of who you are. Once you arrive, you will recognize that it was present all along.

Right now, you have the time for this trip. You have everything your need for this trip. Your bags are packed, which means that everything you need is within. You WILL make the journey with or without your knowledge or consent. Everyone will. Eventually, every spiritual life form will journey to their god self, source self, infinite self…. We thought you may like to know this.

We thought it may help you along your path. We thought it may cut out some of the frustration that you experience. We thought you could use this information as a road map. Now you know where you are going. It doesn't matter which road you take. All roads will lead to the same place. Eventually.

Let us restate: it doesn't matter what road you choose, everyone will end up at the same place. Everyone is made up of the same energy source. Like being drawn by a magnet, everyone—all of life—will return to the source of its origin. We think this is good to know.

Know also that the priest and the whore, the saint and the murder are just names you have for each other. Short-term jobs for people on the path to their source. Best to smile and wave as you pass by each other.

MORE THINGS YOU MIGHT WANT TO KNOW

Time is the teller of all things. That means everything is recorded in time. Everything is available for revisiting. The reason to know this is to aid in your search for truth. When you question who to trust, who to believe, what is the best direction, the answers are stored in the "cells" of your existence. The answers are stored in all of who you are, which is all you have ever been. This isn't as confusing as it may sound. You see, you are similar to a water drop which changes form from evaporation, cloud, rain, ice, snow, ocean, just like you do. Yet your composition stays the same. Water is at least hydrogen and oxygen no matter the form. You are spiritual energy in different form. All of who you are, were, and will be is recorded. That is a truth for you to ponder.

While pondering, let it be known that the best place to look for answers about "you" is inside you. Doesn't that make sense? We hear your concern that you don't know how, and some of you don't even understand what we are talking about. For those of you who are used to using only your brain and what is observable through your senses that would be understandable. For those of you who are used to listening within, you already have an idea of that which we speak. This is all about practice. It isn't a secret that some are allowed to know and others aren't. Can you remember the time before you knew how to drive a car, or swim? Back to the time, when you were afraid and thought you never could? Same thing.

Start by being still. Can you hear the noise inside? Start working with it. Start directing it, shushing the words you don't want to hear, allowing the ones you do. Does it seem as though there are different speakers? If "I" am speaking, who is listening? Keep playing with the voices. Can you hear the voice that sounds like "you" but don't know where the words came from; you didn't "think" those words. This is all you have to do. Listen inside. Eventually, the messages will fine tune. Just like eventually you will drive the car without thinking, or swim with thoughtless pleasure. Same thing. The answers of all time are in you. Start listening.

TIME TRAVEL TO THE BETTER PART OF LIFE

We want to write about a time machine. As we have said, the best time machine is your spiritual energy. It can move much faster and easier that hauling around physical mass. It is also more direct and doesn't need fueling. We recommend using your "time machine" regularly. It's the most efficient way of getting from here to there.

Close your eyes, choose where you want to be, and begin experiencing it. You all do this; might as well make it a conscious and planned trip. Your time machine will show you the better part of life... if you choose.

We say this because we want you to experience the "better part of life." It's all real, just different levels of energy and of knowing. Experiencing the "better part" on an energy level will- if you allow, develop into your physical existence. Time travel to your chosen places will help you increase positive energy on planet Earth. You will be happier, Earth will be a happier place, and your life will probably be more of what you really want. If you ask why you should time travel, the answer is for the joy of it. That is why.

IN THIS TIME OF TRANSFORMATION, EVERYONE PLAYS A PART

The time is now for growth and expansion, the growth of Planet Earth into a new direction. You are here on Earth to assist with this growth. You are here because you chose to enter the physical world at this time, knowing that growth would be going on. Let us make this perfectly clear. Your job, your purpose is for expansion of positive energy. The positive energy includes love, joy, happiness, laughter, fun, appreciation, gratitude... all the high energy frequencies.

We know that you won't be hanging out in high energy at all times. We know that the following generations will spend more time than the current generation in high frequency. We realize that they will be scorned for being happier, more joyful, and loving, and for changing the old rules. They will come into the physical world knowing this on a spiritual level. Let it be. Allow the change. Allow the joy brought to Earth by the next generations. Celebrate with them. The turmoil which Earth is experiencing now is directed toward change, directed towards a new way of being. These are exciting times for Earth, exciting for this generation and all future generations. These times will be recorded and remembered. Be assured... and know that no one died without a cause. Everyone plays a part in this time of transformation. We are grateful for you all.

LEARN TO APPRECIATE YOUR POWER

Now, do not underestimate your power. Do not think of yourself as only one in a million. Think of yourself as the snowflake that became a glacier, the water drop that became an ocean, the grain of sand that became the earth. (By the way, you are) Each and every one of you plays a role and is important to the transition. It is best to know this. Best to know that your physical form is needed for the job of directing energy. You will direct whether or not you realize it, but we think it will be easier if you are consciously aware and can make conscious choices.

Our purpose with these words is to let you know that you are needed and appreciated and to offer guidance and direction. Know that you are loved. Know that you are necessary to the development of planet Earth. Step up and be consciously pleased with yourself. You are loved. The eternal love which you are made of is connected to us. We are you. You and me.

LOVE DOESN'T HAVE A PROBLEM - INTERPRETING THE SCRIPTURES

It is another fine day. Today we will write about Scriptures and verses. Those words of long ago that created a "What did that mean?" Or created everyone's own version of what those words meant. Today, NOW, I want to be very clear with you. No interpretation is necessary. EVERYTHING IS ABOUT LOVE AND KINDNESS. Everything. The core of YOU is love. Use it. Any questions?

Sure there are many questions. Why don't I, he, she, we, they, feel, experience, give and receive love? Answer- as soon as you are ready it will happen. Infinite love is a part of you and always available... always. In the physical world, you are/have been programmed to see the problems. We want you to see the solutions. The solutions are not to create more problems or to wallow in the despair. The solution is in the problem. Always was, always will be.

What does that mean? The solution is to not see the undesired as a problem. See it as an event, or happening. Don't spend time on the problem. It is a physical world problem but not a spiritual or infinite love problem. Live more often from infinite love.

From the source, god, highest frequency, travels the energy of love. There is no problem in this energy. Understand that you ARE this energy. All the other energies which got piled on are what you are living from if you have problems. Go to your strength, your source, your connection. Allow the truth to come through. Allow. Be quiet. This is a lot easier than going through all the other emotions of fear, anger, frustration, depression... before you finally get to peace and acceptance. Your brain is programmed to problem solve, deal with problems, focus on the problem. Do you see the problem? Is it becoming clear? A solution would be to look through acceptance. I didn't say accept a problem, i.e., bad stuff happened. I said to accept a solution without going through all the emotions. I said to accept that the solution is in love, not fear. I said love doesn't have a problem. If you don't want a problem, be in a state of love. Not the "oh honey, I love you type..." I mean the connection to infinite self type of love.

I can hear many people saying "huh," a crisis is going on and you expect me to not react? I say react with loving, peaceful acceptance. That means, do away with all the fear stuff, all the overreaction emotional energies. React from a place of internal peaceful love. Are we getting somewhere with this? It's new information to your brain, but not to what many call a "gut feeling." We call it the truth within.

It only takes a moment to connect to your loving self, especially if you have been practicing.

Now is the time to begin living from your loving self. That is what the scriptures mean. Take the problem to what you call god, source, whole, your inner connection to eternal love. Have I made myself clear on the scriptures?

CONNECTED IN LOVE OR FIGHTING IN SEPARATION

The importance of community. The importance of loving together instead of separating and fighting. Have you had enough bloodshed and violence? Quite the show, quite the drama was put on from planet Earth. The colors of energy shooting out from the planet were a spectacle. When you are finished, there is one way to end. By now everyone should know that the answer is in love. Always was, always will be. If your fight is in the name of God, in the name of love, then there can be no fight. It isn't possible. Love is clean white energy. Pure. God, infinite love, source, the whole of what is... doesn't fight. To fight would mean to have a weakness. Love is the strongest force available. This, of course, leads to an idea that the fight is for a different reason which probably has to do with power. Let me emphasize THE STRONGEST POWER IS LOVE. Your fight will never be stronger. Your fight will never, ever win. Am I making myself clear? The fight can kill which may look like a victory, but it can't maintain life because life is love. Life survives and thrives on love. If you want people to follow, extend infinite love.

Let me suggest that your need for power is because of your belief of separation, a voluntary separation from the whole of all that is, the whole of the strongest energy that goes through all of life- not just on Earth, but the energy of infinite life. That is a big picture. Shrinking it back down to your size creates the image of separation. You versus them. In the big picture, you are them, with your connection to all that is. Imagine viewing the planet Earth from outer space. You would see a oneness. Zooming in, you see the separation. Yet to kill another is to kill a part of the ONENESS. From a seed, became a tree with many leaves. From one source came many people... and all of life. Can you see that *you* are not separate? Your brain belongs to a body, as does the foot, the arm.... You belong to the whole, god, source... as does your neighbor, the next country, the next planet. You do not and will never have infinite power over another. It is not possible. In your short time on Earth in physical form you can create devastation- powerlessness or you can create love- infinite power. Whatever you choose will radiate through time. Not you, just the energy you created. Does that make you feel connected and strong? We hope so. You are, because you are connected to love.

In this exact moment, in the time of now, a new world is dawning, a world of peace. Isn't it about time? Amidst all the chaos and confusion, a new way of being has formed and is working its way to the surface of human consciousness. This new dawning is exciting to us. We welcome an awakening on Earth. It is our pleasure to announce the fulfillment of this dream. It is with much gratitude that we send our praise and our thanks to you all for your participation. Each person played a part. The characters were all on cue. Some of you are consciously aware of the roles being played. Most are not. Either way, each has acted out their part in contributing to peace on Earth. The next few generations will continue the movement... playing out both the positive and negative energies on Earth. Know that everyone is loved, everyone is valued. We appreciate you all.

NOW, CREATE PEACE

We are pleased to be back with another message; a message of peace that you all will be attaining. The message is that you all have the power, as an individual, to create peace. This peace on Earth will never ever be solved any other way. You will always have a choice of extending from your loving self or extending from your fearful (wounded) self. Know that the energy you extend is personal. Know that your energy aligns with other energy. Are you aligning with positive, life-creating energy, or negative, life-depleting energy?

Of course, this will take time to change. Start with awareness. Your brain is programmed, your beliefs are programmed. It will take awareness and practice over time to reset the programmed messages. Be patient and loving with yourself. Be aware of each positive thought and behavior. Be aware of your gratitude. Through awareness, your frequencies can be adjusted.

Start now. Change happens over time. Start with being aware of your attitude, your feelings, your words, and the things you do. Today, create joy for no particular reason. Now, create peace inside of you, no matter what is going on outside. In the moment, breathe into your loving self just because you can. Practice being that which you wish to be- peaceful, joyful, loving. Yes, you can… under any circumstance.

Now, get out of your rut. Do something that will make you laugh inside. If you are about to be executed, look at the executioner and smile knowing that you are connected to your loving eternal self. Do something. Do something that will create a wave of high frequency, loving, and positive energy. Do something while you are in physical form. Your time is now.

Just another note. Miracles are created while you are in physical form. Only YOU can move the mountain.

NOW IS THE BEST TIME TO SHIFT THE ENERGY

The best time to seize the moment is now. Now. The Time Is Now for creating change. The change starts within you. Only You. Take this personally. Is it becoming clear that your responsibility, your challenge, cannot be pawned off on anyone else, or blamed on anyone else? Also, your conditions at the moment do not matter as to when would be a good time for change. As a matter of fact, the best time would be in the worst of times. That is when you will have a lot of negative energy shifting to positive energy. I get it, hard times seem like a difficult time for creating positive energy. But actually, that could be the best time.

Let go of the drama. The more you spin it, the larger it gets. Instead, find your love with in- your infinite love. Your peace and connection are within. Breathe into it. Try... if for only a moment. Find peace in the moment. This is a game changer, a shift of energy. The world thanks you. We thank you. You have shifted energy and increased peace on Earth. Thank you.

PEACE WILL COME WHEN EVERYONE LISTENS TO THE LOVE WITHIN

We think there are many more questions about how to live peacefully in physical form. Do you get that people on Earth are creating their own non-peace? The good news is that if non-peace can be created, peace can also be created. Again, this is a game changer which will require willingness. Most everyone will agree that they are willing and wanting of peace, but not everyone will agree that the change is personal. Make it an "I" am willing to change. Remember that change starts as a belief, and a thought. By doing so, energy is already shifting. The change begins as an invisible energy. The baby is conceived before it is born. We suggest you begin by questioning your beliefs. This will take time. Changing beliefs is a process of looking through old comfortable ways of being which have become accepted without being challenged or updated. It's similar to driving through life, semi-unconsciously on an automatic system that is outdated. It is probably time to update your beliefs.

I hear resistance. "My beliefs are right, are best, are based on..." Yes, we hear you. And we say that if you want peace, open to awareness of a new way of being. Beliefs will continue to change until peace exists on all of Earth. Peace will come from the highest energy frequency. Peace will be an individual choice. Peace will not come through dominance or war. Peace will not come from outdated beliefs of separation. Peace will come when *you* are ready to listen to your infinite love within. There will be no rejection of differences in people once everyone listens to the love within because the same love within you runs through everyone. There is no other way.

CIRCULATING BETWEEN SPIRITUAL AND PHYSICAL SELF

We will be talking about circulation. Around we go with the reasons, the whys. It is all so very simple. That is, we in spiritual form make it simple. Physical forms can create difficulty possibly because physical forms have so many more layers to process through. We would like to help you get more quickly to the source of any matter of concern. Yes, any matter of concern. On an energy field, all concerns can be tracked on a particular energy pathway. All pathways have frequencies. All pathways are illuminated with different hues. That is what makes it easier for us. We don't expect you to see this. In physical form, the senses of touch, sight, sound... are being used then processed with layers of beliefs. Complicated. Let us help simplify. Everyone, from time to time, tunes into their spiritual realm. EVERYONE does this. Everyone hears us. Everyone is guided by both the spiritual self and the physical self. We invite you to strongly develop your spiritual self. Both are necessary. Use them both.

Here we go with the circular, the whys, the hows. You are a spiritual being in a physical body. You adhere to laws of spiritual love and laws of physical experiences. Let's pretend for a minute. Pretend you are an angel having a human experience (truth). Pretend that as an angel physical laws don't apply (truth). Now as an angel having a physical experience, see the experience from your loving angelic place. Oh, we know that the physical reality will be different, but for now, experience it as if you were (are) an angel. For as long as you can, be in your loving place. From here, experience your physical reality. If you are in your loving place, your physical reality will be more peaceful. The noise won't matter as much, the money will be enough, the death will be a peaceful transition, you will survive after the boss fires you... because you are an angel having a physical experience from your loving place. With practice and continuation, this will become easy. In time the whole world will participate. All the negative experiences on Earth will dissipate. The next few generations won't have to work so hard at living peacefully. You are doing it for you, them, for everyone, for planet Earth. You are present as a spiritual energy (angel) in physical form. Don't ignore, don't forget your roots. Practice circulating between your spiritual peacefulness and your physical environment.

THE VOICES WITHIN

We will explain the differences of the inner voice(s). The three of you have been described in different ways with different words. It's all the same no matter what words you call parts of yourself. We hear ego, id, conscious, unconscious, the god within... many names to describe who is speaking, who is listening. You do have a physically conscious part, a middle communicator, and a spiritual communicator, or the connector. You can think of it as the limited, the unlimited and the interpreter. All are of value. Your conscious part is the navigator communicating through the physical realm.

You have a voice for the spirit realm, a voice for the physical realm, and a voice who can communicate between the two. DO NOT presume that one voice is more important than the other. All are necessary.

Now, know that YOU live in more than one dimension. You are in spirit and in physical and there is communication between realms. Could you imagine YOU in any other way but physical and spiritual? Could you imagine not being able to communicate on both realms? No, then acknowledge, accept, and begin living in more peace; the peace which comes from your inner connection to the whole. Live in the whole... in infinite energy, high frequency, joy, love, god.

HEF, High Energy Frequency. Make friends with your inner self. Talk to your inner translator. You are more than five senses. Always were, always will be.

WHO AND WHAT IS GOD

God. The mysterious man of thunder. The ruler of heaven and Earth. The knower, the seer of all. The illusion to physical beings. The battles fought in the name of. Are you ready for some truth?

God is your name for an energy of life. It is the substance of always and forever. This energy that you call God is the energy of pure love, pure life- nothing more nothing less. In the Books when you read, "God is Love" that is correct. God is the pure energy of love and love is the pure energy of life. The problem starts when people want to personify this energy then argue over the differently perceived personifications. Another problem is thinking that this god energy personification lives somewhere out... there. God, the source, the whole of life sexists as an energy throughout all of forever and always. This energy is in every ounce of sand, every mountain, every bug, critter, animal, and pet. God energy is in every human. God energy is a part of every spiritual and physical human. What you call God is the energy of love. God is life. Can you understand this?

If you can believe that god is the energy of love and life which is a part of all, then breathe into the acceptance of truth. Believe also that killings, war, torture have to do with a different energy. Killings, war, torture are not possible with the god energy of love and life. Separation is not possible with god energy. The energy of love and life does not adhere to one and not the other. Impossible. If you are participating in killings, war, torture, etc., then call it by any name other than the god energy of love and life. Name it from a different energy source. There are other energies which do not contribute to life.

Our suggestion is to spend time connecting to the positive energy within you. It is there, of that you can be sure. It is a personal choice. Connect to love, life, joy, happiness or destruction, death, hate, sadness. Choose.

Keep in mind that god, love, life, source, the whole, energy does not come from your brain or your thought-up ideas. It cannot be bragged about, forced on one another, or killed over. It is not possessive, it is not contained. God energy does not separate or divide. God, high energy frequency (HEF), is love, life, long reaching light, clear energy. Your god and mine... and theirs are all the same. Do you get it? Do you understand?

RECORDING YOUR VALUE THROUGHOUT TIME

For the record, for the keeping of the truth, let it be known, that the power of love is within you. Every single one of you and all the animals, including the cockroach, have the power of love, life, god. It can be no other way. People include or exclude. God energy does not. Cannot.

For now, extend kindness whenever possible. Let your high frequency, love, god energy, speak with another high frequency, love, god energy. Start a network of positive energy. Start a network of peace. Include all life forms. Appreciate the plant, the animal, as well as the person. That doesn't mean it is necessary to physically embrace all. But it costs nothing to speak in high energy frequency, to send signals in a high energy, to send and receive kindness, love, joy. The cost is nothing, the benefit is- out of this world. Send and receive frequently... for no particular reason, with no particular expectation. Live from your god within whenever possible.

For the record, we are asking you to grow peace. We are asking you to grow life. You, in physical form on planet Earth, have the power in physical mass to create peace. You have the power to move and expand positive energy. For the record, you are valuable.

FOR A CLEANER HEALTHIER YOU, TAKE OUT THE GARBAGE

And now today, in the dawning of a new way of being, let's start with clearing up some of the garbage within. That negative stuff which is creating sickness, and obstructions in you and on the planet. We think you know by now that everyone, everything has an energy force field. Some people can see it. Some people can feel it. Some call it an aura. Even planet Earth has this "aura" this energy field. This energy comes in colors. You can imagine that the colors relate to wellness and sickness or as we say, to different energy frequencies. These colors, auras, energies are created. They are changeable. YOU are the change maker and the garbage collector. OK, that doesn't sound so glamorous, so you choose a way of expressing a collection of negative energy. Any way you look at it, negative energy doesn't look healthy, feel healthy, or respond in a healthy way. Take your time. Look at the negative thoughts you might have and maybe are not aware of. Listen to your negative conversations, internally and externally. What kind of news do you listen to or watch? Is it positive or negative... we know the answer but do you? And how much negative abuse, garbage, is stored inside of you? Is it time for a cleansing? An emotional, energy, healthy get-rid-of-the-garbage cleansing. We think so. It starts with awareness.

Start by noticing. Take some time, hours, days, weeks, months. Notice how often you experience the garbage of negative energy. Just notice. When you have noticed enough, look at your beliefs. What about your beliefs drew negative energy to you? What are the fear-based beliefs which are in and around you- the beliefs that manifested into negative energy. It's time to dump the garbage and clean out the garbage pail. Disinfect.

This can take a while. The Time is Now to start the process. Cleaning up planet Earth starts with cleaning up an individual. Once the debris is gone, or at least reduced, the fill up of positive laughter, love, joy, happiness can begin. Refill you, the container, with good stuff. Make this a celebration. Celebrate the cleaner, healthier, more joyful you. Take out the garbage.

A GOOD DAY FOR CYCLING, TWIRLING, MOVING ENERGY

It's yet another good day. The goodness comes from within. The day comes from cycles of life energy. That is what your day is. Cycling, twirling, moving life energy. We think that is exciting. We would like for you all to rejoice with us. From time to time, for no particular reason, rejoice. Another day for creating more happy energy. How about right now? How about taking a few minutes *now* to send out joyful, cycling, twirling, moving life energy? No particular reason- just because you can. You are in physical form and have the mass to create the energy of life. We all say thank you!

Let's talk about movement in the direction of life and love. This is science. This is logic. Movement is necessary to maintain life. Movement is life. That is why you are here in physical form. You create movement whether or not you are aware. We want you to become aware because we want you to choose the movement that supports life. We are talking about raising planet Earth to a higher level of consciousness. The time is now. Start thinking about your creation. Think and know that you are important, valued, and necessary for the energy you create. Conscious awareness will be helpful. Conscious awareness is one of the times when you get to use your physical brain instead of your spirit. You get to make choices regarding how you will move energy. By far, beyond any doubt, the best energy to move so that you are maintaining life is the energy of love, joy, happiness, etc. You probably know this. By now, you are probably practicing each day. By now, you are more conscious and creating positive action-energy. We thank you. Earth thanks you. Life thanks you.

YOUR POWER OF SELF INTERVENTION

Time for an intervention. Time to get the ball rolling. It is time for a blast out. Let's get going with a bit of life-saving momentum. The time is now to disrupt, interrupt, get in the way of your negative thoughts. Plan on it. When we say "plan on it" we mean to have conscious awareness of your energy direction. You will be a benefactor. YOU will have a better life. You will experience more peace, joy, happiness with conscious awareness of your energy (feelings). When you are happier, your happy energy travels to others. A chain reaction of higher frequency energy is created. Everyone is responsible and capable of creating this chain reaction. Even when you are alone, practice high frequency energy. The benefit will be yours, plus the energy will travel into your world. Everyone will begin to benefit. We aren't asking you to suffer. The opposite is true. We are asking you to feel and express more joy. The benefits are for you and for the world. If it is peace inside that you want, start an intervention within yourself for the joy.

THE APPENDAGE IS CONNECTED TO THE WHOLE

Do you understand extension? An expansion from a larger source? You are one. So is your neighbor. To understand an extension is to understand yourself and others. While it may appear that you are each a separate individual, you are also extensions of the whole of all. Like tentacles on a sea urchin, like legs on a caterpillar, separate but extensions of the whole. Therefore it is best to work together as a whole, a unit of all that is. All that is… the energy of life. The god, love, source energy… that you are.

We realize that you all think independently. You are created to think in the physical realm. You are created to act as a separate appendage while being connected to all. Each one of you has the ability to create separately, creating life from which you came- love, life, god, source, your beginnings. Can you see that there is no value for you or for your planet to create death, destruction, war, trauma, jealousy, hate… stop. Begin to live from your place of inner peace. It is there. It is present in everyone. It is everyone's individual choice to accept or reject, to live from or away from your connection with the whole, which is always at peace. Are you familiar with that place inside of you? Have you spent time connected to that place? The answer is yes. Everyone has. Everyone may not consciously remember but everyone has lived from the connection to peace, joy, love. Breathe into it now. It is still there. Each of you is still connected to your greater self. We suggest that you stop fighting yourself and others. We suggest a conscious re-connect to your greatest part. Practice often and regularly. Practice connecting to the greatest part of you.

We are pleased that you are beginning to understand. We are pleased that you are beginning to search for the greater part of you. Greater in that it is much larger, and life sustaining. Great that it is YOU in greater self. You are an extension. We are pleased that you are beginning to understand.

YOUR CLOSEST CONNECTION IS WITHIN

Now that you are getting it we will talk about formulating and keeping it. Keeping and acting upon the love within. The God within. You all know about living from the God "out there". Talking to the God "out there". We think this is where a lot of the problems arise. You see. The God out there is also "in there". You don't have to wish upon a star or talk to a great unknown. The God, the source, the whole of all, is a part of you. Tune in instead of out. Let the part of you, the part that you call spirit or soul, let that part live consciously with you. Allow your brain to share consciousness with the god part of you. It can be done. Live from within. That means to allow the connection of spirit and mind. One way of doing this is to allow your mind to accept and allow your mind to believe. Accept that you are whole, you are complete. The god you seek is within. Listen. Your closest connection to all is within.

Take some time with this. Take time to breathe into acceptance. Take time to question. Take all the time you want. Once you tune in and connect, breathe into all you are, experience the homecoming. Experience that which you have always known. You are only an awakening away from peace.

It is time now to discuss the beginnings. The beginnings of time. The beginnings of a new way of life. Now that you are present and ready, this is where and when the miracles of peace and prosperity begin. You see, the miracles happen when the brain connects with the spirit- when the part of you who thought it was the only one running the life meets up with the other part that is running the life. You can call it a divine intervention. Consider it a miracle connection.

YOU ARE LOVED AND GUIDED FROM THE TRUTH WITHIN

Let us begin today with words of a loving connection to self. For everyone, the loving connection to yourself is where you will connect with the greatest truths. You may or may not believe in yourself. That belief is irrelevant as to where the answers are. The beliefs in yourself can be changed. They aren't permanent unless you make it so. If life has caused you to believe in other than yourself, then that can change and it will if you allow. Because YOU are connected to the greatest purest truths, no one can be more important than yourself. It takes time and awareness along with a willingness to believe in yourself and your connection to the whole of all that is. No influence is more important than the influence from your connection to all, to god, to spirit, to self, source... did we get all the names? Whatever you call that part of you, it is greater than what anyone else can say about you. Go to your truth. Go to your source of absolute knowing. Get quiet, and listen from within. Repeat often and regularly.

As we said, this can take time. Some of your beliefs are unconscious. That is to say that you are not aware of all your beliefs and where they came from. Take the time to explore YOU. Stay with the process until you feel the love within. Stay. Continue to explore *the you* past the surface. Spend time in quiet. Notice. Be open to deeper communication. It is there. Always has been, always will be. Whenever you decide to believe in yourself and listen to the love within... it is there.

THE TIME IS NOW FOR YOUR ENLIGHTENMENT

Now is the time to consider awareness of a new age for Earth, the age of the next enlightenment. As you look back through history, you can see that enlightenment was necessary following times of dreariness. Life on Earth is now at a crossing. It is a time to make a conscious decision about survival. Yes, The Time Is Now for awakening. Wake up to thoughts of peace and survival. Doomsday is *not* here, but the path is present with many people trotting blindly forward. We want you to see ahead. Look at the possible outcomes of accumulated fear, disease, stress, greed, hate, war. Look at the accumulated outcome of love, peace, joy, happiness. Feel the difference? Feel the frequencies? Can you feel it internally as an individual? We think you can.

If you can feel it, can recognize the different frequencies, then you can direct the energy. Each of you can direct the frequencies of change. Let's look at a few directions. Speak and listen to what unites. Don't speak or listen to what separates. Choose acceptance of differences. Join with others in the unity of peace. Unity and separation are a good place to start. Join together and survive. Separate and destroy. Your choice, your Time Is Now, while in physical form.

SITUATIONAL AWARENESS

Today we will talk about becoming aware. A big piece of the puzzle is awareness which means seeing the same view differently. We will help. We are certain that most views are seen from your experience(s). Understandable. Now let's look at how you view the experience. You see, experiences are neutral until you apply meaning. Here is where some problems arise over extended meaning, exaggerating and creating drama. Can you see that? Can you see that an experience is neutral until you apply meaning and emotion? Therefore, consider easing up on the dramatic view. Instead, view the situation as a passing experience with many more passing experiences to come. At some time... the present time is good, start viewing experiences with more clarity. This will come from acknowledging that you are much more than the experience. You are bigger, larger than a temporary ever changing place in physical life. You will most likely need to practice awareness. We are sure that you will have many, many, more experiences to practice with. You will have many more times to "see" the view from a different perspective. Whenever you are ready, practice a new awareness-same scene, a better outcome.

REPROGRAMMING AND REWIRING YOUR CIRCUITS

Now we will talk about the time and place for programming messages of peace. The Time, of course, Is Now. The place is right where you are. The programming starts in your thoughts, your ideas, and your beliefs. Think about it for a while. Ponder the idea of a peaceful planet. How will you contribute? Come up with one or two ways that you will contribute. Begin reprograming, rewiring your circuits to include peaceful contributions to the world. By the way, this can be as easy as more smiles to those in need, better words, more laughter... more than your current level. Make it conscious. Become aware of your peaceful contributions. The more you are aware, the better the programming becomes. That is to say, the more you are aware, the more neurons will realign to create a more peaceful YOU. When aligned with other people's little peaceful actions high frequencies become huge. And just imagine what large actions of peace, joy, happiness, and laughter will bring. Let the programming begin all across planet Earth.

THE GOOD MISSION

Today we will talk about energy and your purpose. As we have said, your purpose is to move positive energy, and have negative energy dissipate. This will be a lot easier for future generations. For now, you are here on Earth to make a difference in the flow of energy. We suggest you put thought and consideration into this direction. Really, it is a fun mission, a good mission, a happy mission. We are asking you to do the opposite of suffering. We are asking you to seek more enjoyment while in physical form. CHANGE your programming. Change the view, the beliefs. Beyond a doubt, bad things happen. Beyond a doubt, most of the *bad* things were seen through a negative perspective. Recognize what you have control over. With effort, with practice, you can control your perspective, your behavior, your thoughts, and your beliefs. Start working on it. When you start seeing life as less dreary, life will become less dreary. That is a fact. In time, dreary things will not be as plentiful. That is a fact. Only *you* can create the change from dreary to joyful. We can encourage but you must move the energy. That is a fact. Any doubt?

YOUR HAPPY PLACE IS A HEALING PLACE

Welcome to a new day. Full of surprises. A fun filled day for a great escape. Go to your place of joy. You do have one, right? If you don't have a place of joy, then now is a good time to create that place. If you do have one, now is a good time to revisit and spruce it up a bit. Change the scenery. Grab a universal size paint brush and add some touch-ups to your happy place. This is important. It isn't a joke or a crazy idea. Going to your happy place is creating positive energy for both you and the world. All it costs is time. The Time is Now to create. Close your eyes, and let your thoughts take you away. Enjoy the trip.

Let me add that there are side effects. The first noticeable effect is that you will feel better. Your body appreciates the stress-free environment of a happy place. Your body will respond. Notice the relaxed muscles and tension; notice the digestive track relaxed and flowing. Notice that some or all of your pain dissipated. Your happy place is a healthy place. We suggest you visit regularly for the health and wellness benefits. Take this as a truth. Your healthy happy place is curative, non-invasive, and cost effective. We want you to understand the health benefits of self-curing with peaceful positive energy. Let it flow naturally. While in your happy place, paint a vivid scene. Use vibrant color with lots of mental paint brushes. While you are enjoying your creation in Happy Place, your body is healing naturally, effortlessly. The flow of energy, like the flow of a river, is without concern. Focus on your happy creation, and let the body do what is natural. Go there. Contribute regularly, joyfully, gratefully. Your body thanks you and so does infinite space.

IMAGINE AND KNOW THE ENERGY OF FOREVER

Let's go out on a limb. Let's imagine that you are vanishing in time. We see the shape of you gradually disappearing into a fog. Now imagine that before you are invisible, there is another job to be done. Let's imagine that you come back into view with the strength of the universe pushing you forward. It is your turn to create a miracle, an endless ever flowing breath of energy. The miracle you create will affect earthlings for generations to come.

Now is the time to know instead of imagining. What you are doing on Earth at this moment is creating the miracle of moving energy. We call it a miracle because of the depth and importance of the creation. It is a miracle to think that right now, your energy will be affecting life far into the future. Know that you have the ability to create positive, high frequency, life sustaining, energy. Come back into awareness of your power. You are loved. You are necessary. You are a creator.

The reason we are talking about your time in space is because you are here. You are here- on Earth's space, in a linear, predictable time on a particular calendar, year, day, hour. You are here now to do the job now. Once you are gone, someone else will be doing the job from their vision. We want to express excitement about the job of creating peaceful energy. It is exciting to see the advancement of Earth that will move past the fears. We are looking forward to the happiness, joy, and love that will be in the new Earth.

UNDERSTANDING YOUR PLACE IN FOREVER

Let's talk about the meaning of forever- that endless ever moving space of always. You are here in the middle of forever and always. Yes, we know it is true; your physical self(s) will come and go because the physical is limited. All of observable physical is limited. The mountains, the oceans, Earth... all limited. All subjected to a beginning and end. What is not limited is the power of the source, the whole, the infinite god, which you are a part of. That means YOU are not limited. You will transform, your body will end, but you are a part of forever. This is a truth. Again, it is your choice to believe or disbelieve. We are here to share words; you can accept or reject.

Let's look at the outcome of accepting or rejecting. If you reject, not much will happen. Earth will continue to evolve but just at a slower rate… unless the path of fear in its form of hate, jealousy, greed, anger etc., destroys life. Now, what if our words are accepted? We don't think it is a far reach. We think people already understand eternity, and beginnings/endings. We think people already understand positive and negative energy. We don't think there is too much to understand. What we hope you will begin to understand is your place in all of this. Understand your infinite power. Understand that you contribute to the movement of energy throughout forever. That is what you do. Is it understandable? Good, then let's move on with talk about your place in forever.

We want you all to know how wonderful it is to have you on Earth in physical form. It is our desire for you all to enjoy this time. That is a conscious choice. Even if you are trained to believe otherwise, you can see your experiences as less dramatic. It is OK to giggle, to joke, and to find humor in the rules and happenings on Earth. It is OK to grin when you were going to frown. Training! You have been trained to see failure instead of success… trained to cry instead of rejoice. And there has been a lot of training to doubt when you could have believed. You have been trained to create the negative experiences. What a waste. Now is the time to create a different type of training. Now is the time to train yourself and others to believe, to enjoy, to consciously create the life of your dreams. This will take time and practice. Now is a good time to start practicing. That which you begin creating will benefit future generations… into forever. This is a truth.

Are you beginning to understand that when you complain, frown, groan, mumble about events, you are keeping those kinds of events alive. You are unconsciously doing so by creating energy, a feeling, a thought, a frequency of complaining. Then you get more of what you created. And so does the world. Here is an example. If you are cold and want to get warm, turn the heat up. Put another log on the fire. The heat energy will warm you. If you are getting hot but continue to turn the heat up, you will receive more heat. When you want to cool, stop feeding the fire. If you want undesirable stuff to stop happening, stop feeding the energy that you don't desire. By now, you probably know that re-training means learning to change frequencies. It's that simple.

A CLUE AS TO WHAT THE NEW LIFE ON EARTH WILL LOOK LIKE

Now, we will write about the changing times. A clue as to what the new life on Earth will look like. Let's begin by saying that all of you have this clue. Everyone knows, deep inside, what it would be like for everyone to have food, peace, love. Many of you are working towards this goal. Still, many of you have no idea how this could happen and are unwilling to accept the idea of such a reality. Back to imagining. Imagine that everyone has food and a full belly. Imagine a system of trade that everyone enjoys. Imagine that everyone has learned to feel and share love. Can you imagine it? Can you understand the difference it would make in the world? Just by changing three things, the crime rate would almost disappear. Let your imagination flow. Pick up the speed a bit. It is possible if you can imagine. If everyone starts moving towards abundance for all, it will happen. The seed is imagination. Plant the seed. Nothing more needs to be done until the seed is planted. Did you get the clue?

We hope you are as excited as us about the new world coming. We hope you all will start doing your part of making the changes. Everyone has a part in this creation. You are the snowflake that makes the iceberg. You are the drop of water that creates an ocean. Believe in your power. Plant the seed. Be quiet, let it grow.

ABUNDANCE

This is a good day for remembering that there is enough of everything for everyone on planet Earth. You are not living on a planet of scarcity. You are on a planet with abundance for all. Scarcity is a mindset. Scarcity is a negative way of thinking and believing. What you have or do not have is a direct reflection of beliefs. The simplest, smartest, fastest way to abundance is to know it is present and available for all. No one is singled out or chosen to exist on Earth in poverty. If this is your situation, KNOW that there is an imbalance and an imbalance is not the same as a lack of abundance.

I believe the question then arises as to how balance can be obtained. First, know the truth that there is enough. Change your focus away from lack. Instead, create the belief of knowing abundance. Do you understand? Now, begin experiencing gratitude. If all you have is a tree to sit under, in shade, against an intense sun, express gratitude. Be grateful. Call to you that which you desire. Gratitude is a call- a high-frequency energy call. Do your part to equalize abundance. Ask for your part. Ask by noticing what you have and by expressing gratitude for that which you have. The more you notice, the more you will obtain. Notice the abundance in which you participate. It doesn't matter your current condition. If you are living in poverty, believe in yourself- in your power of creation. Believe that there is enough and you have not been singled out for less. Be grateful and expect abundance.

Next, when you accept your position as having a right to abundance, the wealth will begin to redistribute. Expect what you believe. Believe before you see the evidence. Know that the seed must be planted before the plant becomes visible. Have patience, continue to believe, and continue to be grateful. Become aware of the changes, become aware of the shifts. Become aware of your continued grumbling about not having enough. A process and a transition will develop. Be aware and be joyful. Your part will be done.

No judgments. While seeking abundance, seek the beauty and the joy. Train your eye to see what you want to see, and to be grateful.

Admire the wealth in others. Admire their homes and their gardens. Admire that which you seek. It serves no useful purpose to disdain the beauty and joy of abundance… where ever you see it. The purpose is served through appreciation and gratitude for abundance.

TEAMWORK BECAUSE YOU ARE NOT MEANT TO GO IT ALONE

Welcome back to another glorious day of communication. We are pleased that you are reading these words. We are happy to know that some of you have already taken action. That is to say that the energy has changed for some. That is what we want to happen. We want everyone to experience high frequency more often.

Now, are you getting that there is the "physical you" and the "spiritual you"? That is to say the physical part of you that can be seen, and the spiritual part of you that is less dense and not usually visible. We ask because both are important, and both work best together as a team. If your physical world is unhappy, fearful, angry etc., then you probably aren't working in congruence with your spiritual- less physical self. Both "selves" want the same thing- peace, joy, love, happiness. The physical self usually thinks peace joy etc., comes by obtaining physical comforts. It does, but not always. Make it happen as a team. You aren't meant to live independently or only by the rules of the physical world. You are meant to live purposefully. Your connection to spirit, god, the whole, source, etc., knows purpose and the path. Stay connected, stay happy, stay joyful, and loving within. The spirit within knows of your physical needs, and the spirit within is your best and quickest path to physical joy. Want a house, a car, money, lover, or in other words, do you want to be happy? Join your teammate. Your teammate with less mass knows how to make it happen. Your physical self can move the energy to make it happen. Don't try to be a know-it-all. Any questions?

You are catching on. Good. Let's keep going. There is much more to say about bringing peace to planet Earth- our mission. We are going for it. We are writing about a peaceful transition in this time and this place where and when you are here in this time and place. You have made the decision to enter the physical realm. You are here. This is *your* time to create a peaceful planet. We suggest you consider that all people... all life on planet Earth share the same mission. All is meant to prosper and live. To do so means to enjoy positive energy, which is the energy of life. Negative energy is of non-life. Can you see this? Do you recognize the difference between positive energy and negative energy in relationship to living and non-living? Of course, all energy is living and moving but we are talking about the physical energy of Earth and its inhabitants.

You are here now, on Earth, in physical form, to help Earth maintain life. To do so requires the use of positive energy. The focus now is on increasing positive energy frequencies and decreasing negative energy frequencies. Once you get used to it, once you change your beliefs and behaviors, you and life on Earth will be more happy, loving, and peaceful. We want to emphasize peaceful. You can think of it as your mission. Your most important mission while in physical form on planet Earth is to move the energy in a positive direction. You move the mountain, love is the direction. Let me repeat, Love is Life. Equal. One exists as a part of the other. One cannot exist without the other. Your purpose is to keep the energy of love flowing- the energy of love which encompasses joy, happiness, laughter, fun.... your purpose. I think we have made this very clear. Shift your beliefs. Create that which is intended.

REWIRE THE PROGRAMMING

If you are saying, thinking, believing, that life is hard, life sucks, people are mean, stupid.... rewire the programming. Or if you say, think, believe, "I am poor, lonely, living in lack" we say, rewire the programming. "It hurts, love hurts". Rewire the programming. Similar to a radio, if the sound is distorted or too high, too low, too much static, then rewire the programming. Make adjustments. Create a clean resonating sound. Simplify. Cut to the chase. Debrief.

Now, start clean. Begin with a clean state of consciousness. Begin with an awareness of yourself inside and out. Understand that you are much more than you realize. You are the alpha and the omega. The beginning and the end. You are also the voice in the middle of a transformation. Yes, you are.

SEE HEAR

It is time for a new vision. You can see you are beginning to see your place in the transformation of Earth's energy. It is good. We are pleased. Now is the time for choices and decisions. Now is the time to begin consciously moving in the direction of your desire. Yes, of course, this direction has always been a part of you... unconsciously maybe, and now is the time to purposefully "be" in the movement of peace, of enlightenment. Wake up, clear your vision, and "see" your purpose. See that you are all that is necessary for continued life on Earth. You, an individual. You are important to the role of peace on Earth. It wouldn't do much good to look at another person and expect change. The other person may be looking at you, consciously or unconsciously. Be peaceful. Reflect the peace so that the other person will pick up on and connect with, bits of your energy. A little at a time, peace will be picked up. The energy of peace starts with YOU. Do you see?

What do you hear? What are you listening to? It might be time to retrain your ears for sounds of peace. Stop the rumble of discontent. Straighten out the waves of peace. The peaceful energy waves travel a lot further and faster than rumbling discontent. Listen to what you want to hear. Listening inside is always a good choice. Listen to words of truth. We have your interest at heart. Words of peace will not be blaming, hurtful, disrespectful. Words of peace are not words of separation. Know this. Become enlightened. Listen to peace. All else is just rumbling.

THE PROCESS BEGINS INTERNALLY THROUGH AWARENESS.

Begin the process internally. With the decision made that establishing peace is a part of your mission, now is the time to take action. We suggest that you begin by monitoring your awareness. Become aware of your thoughts. Notice when you are thinking in high frequency and low frequency. That really means to notice when you are thinking positive, life-sustaining thoughts or negative, life eliminating thoughts. Your thoughts are energy waves that travel. Your thoughts create. Every thought has power. Notice which ones you cling to and convert into beliefs and which ones you cling to and convert into actions. With practice, become conscious. Know that you are making a decision, whether or not you planned to.

Once awareness has begun, healing begins. All of planet Earth will begin to heal once individuals become aware of their positive and negative thoughts. Once awareness happens, choices can happen. Choose life, choose peace. Become aware of your power- your strength.

THE PATH TO PEACE

Now, let's look at some paths of peace. We think that everyone will agree on some level that peace is the preferred direction. Naturally, trouble begins with selecting the path. We tell you, there is only one path for you and others to take- the path of love. That is all. That is the only path of survival for Earth. It is important to know this. Remember, when we speak of love, we speak of eternal love, god love, the source of all life. Really, the word LOVE needs to be changed but for now, it is the only word we have to express the highest, strongest, most powerful energy of all. Get it out of your mind that love is a weakness or that it is only for a select, physical form. Get it in your mind that we are talking about the greatest sustainable life force which is a part of your makeup and a part of every single thing. Powerful. Imagine. The path is high frequency, love is the highest. Joy, happiness, playfulness, etc., all fall in line. We don't think it is difficult to choose the right path. We think the difficulty is in choosing the paths that separate and divide- those paths which create negative energy. Make it easy on yourself and for everyone else. Choose the path of highest frequency. Be the path, be joyful.

TIME FOR BEGINNINGS, TRANSITIONS, EVOLVING

Today we will write about the time for beginnings. As we have said, now is the time of transition, the time of a new awakening. People on earth are evolving into the next enlightenment. To evolve means to change and adapt to a different way of being. You see, the old path has too much negativity which destroys. The new path is based on love which is synonymous with life. That is your choice- positive or negative, life or extinction. Wake up Earth. Live, love, celebrate, laugh, be joyful. The movement has begun. Join in... start now. Today.

Do we need to tell you how to enjoy life? Do we need to tell you how to embrace instead of destroy... to love instead of kill? Do we need to tell you that greed is not a high value? No, we don't need to tell you. The truth is inside of you because you are life which means that you are love. Tune in to that part of you, listen to your truth. EVOLVE!

Let's look at some specifics. Drugs, Money, Power.

We aren't going to condemn. There will be no punishment, no blame, no righteousness on our part. We do have suggestions though. Follow the path.

Drugs, both legal and illegal are ways of coping physically. There is no purpose in condemning and killing drug users or drug enablers. Our suggestion would be to stop giving it such negative attention. If the user asks for help, then give it. If not, let the user find their way... struggle to find their path. Offer love, kindness, and support just like you would for depression, heart disease, diabetes. Let the user choose to accept or reject your offer. What we are saying is that judgment, imprisonment, or murder is not the solution. Yes, we understand that it is difficult to watch addiction- and illness. Stop watching. Stop judging. If you are a user or if you know a user, your paths are the same. Choose to participate- or not. No blame, no shame.

Money, we get that it buys stuff for physical life. We get that it is an exchange program for goods and services. We also get that life on Earth will be easier when everyone has equal exchange... and it will. That is the direction of change. Poverty will disappear at the same time beliefs of hoarding disappear. There is enough for all. Change the rules, change the game.

A shift in power comes with a shift of beliefs. If you think someone has more power than you, it will be true. If you think you are as powerful as anyone on Earth, then it is true. You see, "power" is a human thought up conception. It is a way of believing. Power is a belief. A belief is a power.

The concepts of drugs, money, and power are all frequencies of energy. Change the belief- change the frequency.

INTEGRATING INTO ONENESS

Now, let's move on. We want to revisit the ideas of integration. The idea of oneness for planet Earth– one Earth, one love. The liveliness of Earth is equal to the love of its people. The sickness of the earth is equal to the low frequency of its inhabitants. From our view, the planet Earth and all encompassed within its sphere is one. One planet in many life forms like one tree with many leaves. It is time to start acting as one purpose.

The same physical matter is a part of all. The same energy frequencies are a part of all. The same source, god, whole, is a part of all. It will be a lot easier for everyone to live from the idea of *the belief of one,* than to live from the *belief of differences.* It is easier to change the focus to seeing togetherness instead of separation. Once people start seeing the oneness, understanding the oneness, beliefs will change to oneness. That means that one purpose will develop- the one purpose of expanding positive energy waves of life. We think you are beginning to see. We think that you are beginning to understand that everyone is a leaf on the same tree of life. Genetics?

There is more to say. We can say with absolute sincerity that life/ love is worthwhile. We can say with sincerity that you, YOU are an honor to us. Be yourself, laugh with yourself; we applaud your time in physical presence, thank you. Thanks for moving the mountain to a higher place. Thanks for moving in a spiritual direction. Thanks for listening to us. It is time for evolving into oneness.

TIME OUT FROM YOUR PHYSICAL ADVENTURE

Now, let's talk about time out. Taking the time out to rethink, re-group. We want you all to reconsider your daily chores. Your daily job is to expand positive energy within your current daily position. Every position for humankind is a good place to expand positive energy. In your best, most secure, most wonderful place, radiate that joy of being there. If you are in the worst possible place, life threatening, dangerous, escape the physical condition by going inside, to find your connection to love. It is there. It is within at all times. Connect to it. Wherever you are, whatever your job, take time to connect with the love within. It isn't necessary to stay in this spiritual place. We understand that you are living a physical life in a physical place, and the physical body needs to be cared for. We suggest that you pop in and out of your spiritual place, your loving place. Whatever job your physical body is in, take time to pop into your spiritual place. Work from there as much as possible. By doing so, your physical work will be much more tolerable. It is without doubt that your physical world will change as people begin to live from both their spiritual self and their physical self. Keep in mind that the spiritual self is where the good stuff is… the joy, happiness, and fulfillment that you seek. It is there to help you with the more difficult physical world. Your most difficult journey is where you most need the loving, spiritual connection. Practice. Your most wonderful adventurous daily activity is a great place to express gratitude. Practice. Then, start noticing the changes in you and your world. Take a time out to go within.

TEACHING AND LEARNING THE NEXT WAY OF BEING

Now is the time to step up to responsibility, to create from a place of intentional awareness of peace. It is time to direct energy with knowledge of the direction. Everyone directs energy. Everyone can learn and teach awareness. That is to say that everyone can learn and practice directing energy. Then, everyone can teach others. Teach. Nurture the next generation. Let them know that they are loved and that strength comes from within. That is to say, let them live from their spirit, not from where they are told to live. Guide and direct them as we guide and direct you without judgment or condemnation. Look for the joy within, and nurture it. Usually, the spirit of a child knows the path. Watch them and learn. They will teach you in return for you teaching them. Allow this.

Further, we will say more about parenting. First, we want you all to know that the child is sent through your physical form because that is the way of creating a new life. That does not mean ownership. That means a unit of physical protection has been formed. You all may think ownership in a legal way, yet spiritually, no one can own another. Everyone can be a guide. Age doesn't matter. Everyone is equal with the ability to guide and teach. At every age, there are lessons to be taught and learned. We suggest acting with mutual respect for the guidance in everyone at every age. Often the problem is an unwillingness to follow... to see that a message is being presented. Often the assumed authority feels dominant. Because of this attitude of dominance, the person is unwilling to recognize the equality of all spiritual beings in human form. We are talking about respect. This lesson is about mutual respect for all of life. Sometimes you are the student sometimes you are the teacher... always.

A BACKLASH FOR ALL

It is about time to consider the effects of a backlash in history. This backlash, this history, is about moving into the future armed with love instead of fear. The backlash is from power, greed, war, poverty, and separation. The backlash is about love, joy, happiness, prosperity, and gratitude. The backlash is saying that dividing people into those who have and those who have not, is destroying life on Earth. Eventually, like in the game of monopoly, the masses would fall. History has been there many times. The Time is Now to become a backlash. It is time to recognize that love, respect, and joy for EVERYONE are important. Rewrite the rules. Wake up Earth. Everyone can win; everyone is important. Everyone has the job of creating infinite positive energy. Change the rules to make this happen. Change the rules so that no one becomes a beggar living on the streets. We want you ALL to recognize that it is the responsibility of everyone to make the rules that will help everyone. Change the rules so that there is no first class or bottom class. Change the rules. Create a backlash of infinite love and equality for all. The history of those at the top and those at the bottom is unbalanced. It is time to balance. It is time for a backlash of love for all.

Imagine future generations. Imagine them living together peacefully. Can you imagine them living peacefully without separation? Can you imagine a flourishing planet for everyone? Try. Practice. Celebrate the vision.

This does exist in other places. It will exist on Earth also. The only way for life on planet Earth to survive is to live together peacefully. This can be achieved with togetherness... oneness of life on Earth. Oneness starts with a vision, a thought, and then a belief, the belief of equality, the belief that everyone has the purpose of creating positive energy frequencies. If everyone has the opportunity to achieve this purpose, then all of Earth wins. Stop making it difficult. Stop creating separation. Imagine a backlash that allows everyone the ability to create infinite love.

THE SEASON OF CHANGE

Let's talk about the season. This is the season of change, growth, and development. The time is now for a new planet Earth to wake up and evolve. Gone are the days of competition to survive. Let me say that again. Competition to survive. The time has come to an end when some people have all they want while others struggle and die. We are saying, wake up. Look around. Look at the mansions and the people in the gutter. Look at how some people are poisoned so that other people have unnecessary richness. Yes, we know that everyone can live in abundance. Everyone can create abundance. We are talking about leveling the field. People of Earth won't survive in a class system of the rich and the poor. That path will eventually end life. No, everyone is equal in a universal, spiritual law. Everyone is here for the purpose. It is time for everyone to participate in the purpose of expanding positive energy. The change will take place over the next generations. Your children and grandchildren will spread the resources for everyone... without judgment. A new system will assure that everyone is cared for. Accept this. Accept that a change is here. Everyone is first class.

THE MINDSET OF EQUALITY

We are ready. Are you ready for the next adventure? We'll streamline this. In preparation, imagine a time of freedom from financial worry. Imagine a time of prosperity. The time is coming when everyone is peaceful. No more war, or fighting over stuff. You see, all of that "I've got to have, even if you have not," will end. Doesn't that sound peaceful? The fights are over possession and ownership. The solution is to realize that everyone is powerful and everyone can have, and everyone contains the same highest energy frequency. The answer is to change the mindsets of both the have and the have-not people. Blame isn't going to do any good. Both the rich and the poor contribute to the same issue of equality. Change the mindset. Change the beliefs so that the energy will change into abundance for all. Do this for yourself and for the future of Earth. It is possible to live together peacefully by removing the competition to thrive or to survive. There is no glory in greed or poverty. There is no "better" no "worse" person. There is a human with a spirit on physical Earth, here to create the high frequency of love, life, god... synonymous words love, life, god. Allow each other to spread the joy and the gratitude. Allow kindness for oneself and for one another. Practice. Start the mindset for the next generations.

PAVING THE PATH TO PEACE

The path is paving the dusty road. Civilization is in the next phase. We are all on the path, whether or not you realize it. This is an exciting time in the history of life. Think of yourself as pioneers on the next frontier. Like when the automobile was invented, and the telephone and the computer, the world changed. Those were new frontiers for people. Technology evolved, and spiritual beings are evolving too. Your part in all of this is to pave the path of awareness. That means to open your minds to new beliefs and new ideas. To start looking at solutions of peace, start believing in the possibility of peacefully co-existing. We aren't asking for much... just for you to become aware of your thoughts, beliefs, and actions. We want you to look at your contributions- and you all contribute. The Time Is Now to pave a path to peace. Each one of you, individually, look at your contributions to love, joy, happiness, and your contributions to fear, hate, war. Look at the results of your words. Notice if they divide and separate human kind. That means do you speak of hate, judgment, belittlement, of others? Can you see the oneness in us all? Can you see others from the place of pure energy that runs through you and everyone? Can you understand life from the place of your heart... your infinite love? That is the path to pave- an understanding of all life from your infinite self to theirs. Practice paving the path each day. Practice understanding and believing in peace. Pave the path joyfully.

DISSECTING THE CURRENT PHYSICAL REALITIES

Good day for a new adventure into the outer realm. We will talk about dissection in the process of re-creation. In order to create the peace you want, that everyone wants, the rules will have to change. To change the rules means to look at "what is." Dissect the current physical realities. Take a closer look at the way physical life is working for Earth.

From our position, we see all the colors of energy. We see the pockets of darkness and the places of light. We see the mixtures of energy throughout. We want to raise the light, diminish the darkness. This is your purpose; it will also be your joy, happiness, and peace. As we have said before, your colors, your energy reaches far into the outer realms. Light, love energy reaches furthest. Dark energy is like a clog in the drain… the arteries… the intestines. It doesn't travel as far. Can you see the problem? Can you see the name-calling, yelling, anger, bombs, prisons, as contributing to blocked energy? This is the dissection process. Look at what energy you are creating. See the contribution from each of you. World leaders, judges, ministers, paupers, street dwellers all create energy. Become conscious. The first act of dissecting the problem is to see your contribution.

JUDGMENTS

We will talk about judgments. We think it is important to separate the idea of differences from judgments. You may notice differences and you may judge one to be different from another, short, tall, overweight, underweight. The problems begin when a value is placed on the differences- good, bad, acceptable, unacceptable. We suggest noticing differences without applying a value. Notice the differences. Accept variety. Value all. Practice. Is that clear to you? Do you understand the value of acceptance instead of rejection? Do you get that a judgment carries an energy frequency? The energy comes from the person giving judgment. Know that the type of energy you are sending towards others is about you, the sender. The value judgment is about you, not about those you judge. Understand the difference.

DWELLING IN FOREVER

We are pleased that you are here and in a good space for more words. This time our words will be about dwelling in forever. Some people on Earth call this dwelling in the house of the Lord or dwelling with forever family or with their chosen god. We call it "Dwelling in Forever." By any name, the place of forever is a part of you all. Everyone is made up of the energy of infinite life. Your energy will glow always. There are different versions of your energy. That is to say that you can be surrounded in physical form or to state more clearly, your spiritual self will visit many realms. You are a "constant" in motion. You will never, never, poof into nothingness. Our suggestion is that you all learn to enjoy your rendezvousing self. See your physical self for the fun it can be. Remember, most of the anguish you experience is just drama. Like when a child falls and scrapes a knee, brush it off and keep going for adventure. Yes, yes, yes, we hear your dramatic words that your experiences are more than a scraped knee. We say that in infinite time, your experiences of joy are what matters. Your creation of positive energy is what matters. The child's scraped knee is less important than the child's adventure. What we want you to know is that your adventures are creating energy. Resonate with positive energy. Send and receive positive energy. Shine as often as possible. Dwell in the house of love, which is really an infinite space.

EQUALITY OF ROLES

Now it is time to talk about the pros and cons, the for and the against of equality. There is much to say about equality but the truth is everyone is equal on a forever spiritual journey. In physical form, hierarches have been established. Of course, you know that those at the top are usually unwilling to give up their position. And of course, those at the bottom are usually unhappy about their position. Each and every person is playing a role while in physical form. No one has to be stuck in their role. Before birth, there is somewhat of an awareness of the role you will be playing, a general idea. The choices you make during physical form will influence and direct the path of your role(s). You always have a choice to accept or reject your position. No super power assigned roles for life on Earth.

Now let's say that you are rich and royal. You probably decided this role before you were born. As history has shown, everyone is capable of moving in or out of rich and royal. The same is true for low-level laborers. There is a purpose, and everyone still has a choice to move in or out of the position. The choice is to believe in you. Let go of a belief that others placed you in your role. Believe in your power to direct your path. Now, if you really want to argue that you didn't choose the path, go inside- into your inner spiritual self. Listen. Find your personal role. The one you most fit into. The role you are most comfortable with. And know that roles are flexible and ever-changing. In this physical life form and in many others, sometimes you will be royal, other times you will be cleaning up the mess. We suggest you love yourself and be joyful with each role you assume. Everyone equally chooses their roles.

LIVING BY INFINITE TRUTHS

We will talk about the discovery of truths and how to do this. You see, a truth is transparent. That means everyone can see into it. Everyone has the ability to look deeper into truths which govern all of life. The truths everyone wants to know will bring peace for everyone. Doesn't this make sense- that a truth would not be for some without being for others? One way to determine if what you are saying or doing is a truth for all would be to ask, is it good for all? Possibly a lot of rearranging might have to be done before getting to a truth. Possibly a lot of rearranging of thoughts, beliefs, actions, and plans would need to happen before getting to a truth. An infinite truth, a god truth, is always about love/life which is expanding positive frequencies. In order to move forward as one sustained planet Earth, its inhabitants must look for truths which are true for everyone. This will certainly be a process that will last for many generations. Once accomplished, Earth will be the utopia, the nirvana, the heaven that is now a vision, a dream, a thought. We want to say that this vision is a reality. It is a reality in the making. YOU are playing in this role of dream maker. Imagine a truth much larger, much grander in purpose. Start living by it.

Once people start living by a truth for all, there will be no need for prisons, police, or violence. Laws, law makers, and law keepers will change. The poor and the rich will be on common ground. Can you see that much of the crime is because of those who have and those who have not? There is a universal truth that states, "There is enough for everyone." Now is a good time to start thinking and believing in this truth. Now is the time to begin.

ACCEPTING FOREIGN AFFAIRS

Today we will write about foreign affairs. Foreign meaning affairs that we know little about, affairs that are not consciously experienced, affairs which are a part of us all but possibly foreign to our conscious brain. Those are the foreign affairs foreign to the conscious brain. You see, our brain knows through the five senses of hearing, seeing, tasting, touching, and smelling. That is the conscious part. The "foreign" part of us is the spiritual part, the unconscious... for many but not all of us. Here within everyone are the affairs of love, life, and eternity. It is our playground of forever. We want you all to experience this loving playground... often. The "foreign" affairs of you have a lot to offer. The foreign affairs are not mysterious voodoo places. And for that matter, neither are foreign countries on Earth. It would be best for everyone to accept that which is unfamiliar. Accept that there are other ways of being, other possibilities to learn about. Most importantly, accept that if you are seeing, hearing, touching, tasting, or smelling life that is low frequency, which is separating, blaming, judging, then consider accepting a foreign affair of peace, love, life-foreign to you maybe but not foreign to eternity. This place is alive and well within every life form. All you need to do is become familiar and embrace foreign affairs, your guides through forever.

YOUR HEAVEN ON EARTH

Good day. We are geared up and ready to speak. It is Time Now to discuss a new movement, a grand and glorious movement for planet Earth and all life forms. To describe this imagine peace, serenity, love, happiness, and joy- everywhere. Imagine your heaven. Can you see it? Can you experience your heaven for a few minutes? What if you could experience it every day for as long as you want? Of course you can. You have everything available that you will need. As you "think" of your heaven on Earth, you are actually creating your heaven. In time, your thought processes will begin to change from negative, depressing, angry, worry thoughts to your newly created heavenly thoughts. This will take some time so make space for the good time thoughts. All your head has to do is schedule a time then get quiet, get out of the way and allow. Your "heart" can take it from there. Your heart, otherwise known as spirit, knows how to create this heaven in you. Part of your work will be with keeping the brain from interrupting with all the buts... it will create; all the interruptions and excuses that interfere with the peaceful process. When the interruptions happen, tell them- not now. Tell them that they can speak after the peaceful heavenly moments. Teach your brain to take turns with your heart. That really means, teach your physical self to take turns with your spiritual self. Got it? Good! Start practicing the creation of your heaven on Earth.

LIMITS

Now we will talk about the limits of your physical world. Part of the annoyance of people in physical form is because of limits. You may not recognize it as such but still, it is about being limited. As we have said, there are no limits in the spiritual world. We suggest that people on Earth begin living with fewer limits. How about living with the limits set by physical form plus a few of people-made limits? Physically speaking your body has limits which you can't avoid, one of which is death. Your thought up human-made limits can be avoided. We don't understand why you would place limits that impose on freedom. Freedom is much more enjoyable than limitations. We suggest that you open your minds, your thoughts to ideas of freedom for everyone. That means stop making laws and rules of limitation. Allow. Allow the freedom to live fully whenever possible.

You see, there comes a time to place freedom above limits. Freedom creates a high frequency while limits create low frequency. We are talking about imposing laws, rules, or limits on others. Having power over another. We agree that there is a time and place for limits, for rules that regulate. What we see too much of are rules, laws, and limits that create fear-based behavior, not love-based behavior. What we are asking is that you think about the consequence of your rules and laws which create limits on others. Instead, create freedom. Allow. Honor each other by allowing personal freedoms. When in doubt, choose freedom.

AN ARMY OF WARRIORS

It is time to discuss the pros and cons of building an army. We suggest that you build an army of do-gooders, an army who will fight for freedom. Build an army who recognizes peace. Build an army who marches forward with tolerance. You will build by joining others in the peace movement. Your peace movement army and your gun carrying army, both fight for peace. Both armies expect peace to be the outcome of the fight. The real outcome with guns is separation through dominance versus coming together in peace. The trophy is peace; the prize is a better world. Pros and cons. Dominance will always create more wars.

With that being said, it is time to create peaceful warriors. It's time to create warriors who will unite instead of divide. Now is the time. Now, while life on Earth is still here. As we have said, changing the minds of warriors into peace keepers will take generations. The people of Earth are off to a good start. The peace energy is buzzing with conversation and action. Others will be joining in. Still, others will be learning about peace but won't be ready to join. All is well. All is how it should be. Move forward either for or against peace.

EVALUATING YOUR LIFE

Arrange for a new beginning. It is time to make arrangements for this better world that is being created. Evaluations are necessary. Start with your present situations. Evaluate what you do in the world today. Evaluate your beliefs. Is your life about joy? Is your job about joy? If you could change it, what would you do? The truth is that you can change it, create it, and be it. Take the opportunity to think about your life- to listen inside. Dwell on the things you like. Spend time thinking about what makes you happy. Begin dwelling.

Now, have you been dwelling on what makes you happy? Good. Probably all you needed to do was to go inside and tap into the happiness already present in you. Tap in and allow the happiness to surface and surround you. It is a choice. Tap in and allow or don't. Remember, that the frequency you choose is what will come back to you.

Please, please see life as an adventure. Life is a playground full of fun opportunities. Re-train your brain. Experience the joy. This is your time to create joyful waves of energy.

CONGRATULATIONS
Go for the gusto. You have no reason to hold back. Well, you might have man-made reasons but there are no reasons in spiritual infinite time. While you are in body, experience the infinite you. Experience the never ending joyful, loving, fun part of you. This is your time.

The best way to do this is to know that life doesn't have to be so dreary. Life isn't supposed to be dreary. It is meant for you all to be in body and produce positive growth energy. Coming is a new way of thinking, a new way of being. This new way will bring joy for everyone. The past ways of thinking were about individual struggle and competition for survival. It is over. The new way of being is about living together in oneness instead of separation. Joyful times for all. Congratulations Earth for getting to this next way of existing.

TOGETHER IN BEAUTIFUL DIFFERENCES
Today we will write about togetherness which is the act of believing that we are all connected. Therefore, we are all together as one. Your roots and theirs, all go to the same source. Doesn't it make sense to treat each other as part of the same whole? Let's talk about getting past the differences. Imagine being a part of a string of colored lights wrapped around a pole. These lights all blink or flash at a different time in different colors and on different sides of the pole. All the lights are connected to the same cord which is connected to the same

electrical outlet. Mysterious to some is the outlet's source of energy. Mysterious because it can't be seen. It is hidden on the other side of the wall and beyond. But electricians understand where the energy comes from.

It would not make sense for a light at the top of the pole to think it was better than a light at the bottom. Nor would it make sense for one light to get angry with another because it didn't flash in unison or one light was flashing red while another flashed green. The pole is Earth, the lights are life forms, and the cord is our spiritual connection, to endless power. Don't put out each other's light. You are all in this together, and beautifully different.

YOUR POWER OF POSITIVE CREATION

Another good day for sharing words. Today we will talk about power. The power in all of you comes from the same source. Do you find it enlightening to know that "you" are equally important as "him, her, or them?" Once you start living with this confidence, you will be able to achieve your purpose much more successfully. Remember, your purpose is to create frequencies of positive energy. This is difficult to do if you think of yourself as less than another- consciously or unconsciously. This is an invitation to bring awareness to yourself. Be aware of the wonderfulness of you. If you can't see your wonderfulness, then look in a different direction. It is your choice to see in you that which you want to see. Look for the good stuff. Bring a lot of awareness to your goodness, and then be grateful for seeing that part of you. There! You did it. You increased your positive frequency. You and the universe will benefit from your power of positive creating. Go ahead-rejoice. Smile, dance, sing or laugh aloud. It's all powerful. We thank you.

It is time again to talk about RULES. It is much easier to talk about the rules of infinity. Infinite rules are easy to get along with. The most important infinite rule is LOVE. Love is most important because it is life. Without love, there would be no life. We encourage you all to make rule number one the most important in your life. Not just about a loving relationship, but a deep sense of love for all. Work at it. Take time to develop a sense of love for all. This will take practice. Try to experience this a bit every day.

BY-PASS THE STORM ON THE WAY TO YOUR DESIRE

Today is a good day to talk about weathering the storm. This storm will be about indecision. We are aware that it is sometimes difficult to decide on a future, unseen event. All the "what ifs" pop up. What if the decision was wrong? What if you don't make a decision? What if you are afraid to change your beliefs and change the world? A suggestion would be to look far enough out. What would you want to see? The first decision would be to look at what you want to see. Next would be the decision to start in that direction. Is this getting a little easier for you? You see, decisions are about seeing a direction. It doesn't matter what you are deciding about, look in front of the decision to see what you want to see. Now, imagine that for a time you want to see peace. Good, we hope you do. Imagine that you want to participate in a peaceful movement. Good, again we hope you will. And finally, imagine the outcome. A part of the decision might have been because of fear. What if people look at you as if you are wrong, or they doubted you, or your beliefs appeared to be too different from others in your group? What if you are afraid to speak up? Because of your "what ifs" your decision becomes more difficult. You might have created the storm that blinds you. It would probably be easier to look past the storm and into the result you want. Look forward towards your desire. We think the point is made. You don't need to create stormy weather on the way to peace.

THE BIG PICTURE OF SPACE ENERGY

Now we will talk about space energy. That place in the great expansive unknown sky. It really is a thriving community. Space. The time has come for people on Earth to become more aware of a larger existence. You are a part of the whole; you are not the whole of all. When the time comes for visits, which will mostly just be awareness, a loving non-fearful reception is recommended. Awareness means being able to see, hear, experience past your current realities. Awareness would be having the ability to communicate consciously on an energy connection. Some of you can understand but others won't while in this embodiment. In time, the ability to connect without using physical body parts will become normal. For now, awareness of the possibilities is enough. The seeds are being planted. The larger picture will become clearer. It is truly an amazing place- the big picture.

CREATING CHANGE THROUGH AWARENESS OF BELIEFS
Knowing and believing. Knowing is the art of conscious believing. That is why we want you all to look at challenging your beliefs. We want you to recognize where your beliefs came from and how they were instilled in you. Spend some time thinking. Think about a subject and notice your beliefs filter in. Where did the beliefs originate? Is it time to keep them or change them? If you are looking for a peaceful environment, everyone- *everyone*, must challenge their beliefs. It is certain that this will take a long time. Now is a good time to begin. We are telling you this because a different wave of energy is sweeping over Earth. It is time for Earth to have a conscious awakening. What we are asking is for willingness to accept that peace is the future. To get there, everyone must become aware of personal beliefs. The first stage is awareness. With awareness, change happens. Know this.

Getting from here to there is a choice. The choice is to stretch your comfort zone, whether you are happy or unhappy in your zone. Let's say that you are pleased with your abundance. Good for you. Let's say that you are unhappy with your position in life but see no way to progress. Not so good. No matter your position, know that you have the power to create by becoming aware of your beliefs. Create conscious awareness of all you are. Have conscious awareness of your greater potential. "Here" is your present position; "there" is the position that comes from a changed belief. The new world will experience a deeper level of consciousness. The next generations will live from a place of deeper knowing. It is time again for life on Earth to challenge beliefs, begin living from new truths, and let go of archaic thinking. The time is now and the beginning is upon you. Allow.

A micro level is where the changes will come; a level so small that it can't be seen. An energy pulse. That is where the change begins. The desire which leads to the reality begins with a connection of two or more frequencies. It isn't complicated. Two or more charged circuits come into contact producing a reality. A stroked flint can produce a spark. Whether you want abundance or peace or love, the change will happen when you combine belief with infinite power. That is a truth. Now if a group, or a community, or a country, share the same belief, it will happen. Let's say that the country believes in abundance for all. Laws will be made that benefit abundance for all. Because some people don't agree, it may not become a reality. The place to start is with the individual. Each of you creates a belief of abundance. Join with each other and abundance will happen. It is that simple.

ADJUSTMENTS
We will talk about making adjustments. Preparing for an adjustment starts with a thought. The adjustment will happen, but it will be easier if everyone is prepared and willing. This adjustment is about connecting to the whole of you. Right now is a good time to understand the greater part of you. Once you do, adjustments happen. Internal adjustments that change your frequency will draw to you a better existence. It's science. It has to be. Draw unto you that which you seek by making adjustments in your thoughts, attitudes, and beliefs. Desire peace. Now isn't that simple?

Begin to make adjustments by making a choice. You see, once you look at your choices, you'll recognize the differences between those in your head and those in your heart. That is another way of saying your physical self and your spiritual self. Choices from the heart/spiritual self comes from your connection to the whole- god, source etc. When it comes from the whole, it benefits all. We are saying that you can have whatever you want. So can everyone else if you make adjustments from your heart that benefit you and everyone. Do you get it?

KNOW OF YOUR GREATNESS

Today is about sovereignty. Each of you is sovereign because of your connection to the greatest power. We want you to understand this. It is important to know your greatness. Your actions will be different once you understand your greatness and your connection to love, source, god…... Imagine how much violence would decrease if everyone knew of their sovereignty, their connection to the highest power. Imagine knowing that you- yes YOU are great, excellent, and certainly important to the whole. You are the great generators of positive energy. It is YOU who will light up the world with greatness and power. We aren't talking about a mystical someone in the great unknown. We are talking about your connection to god, source, love, the whole. Love is life. God is life. You are life. Act from that place inside of you. Act out your connection. Be proud. Because you are a spirit in physical form on the physical plane, we honor you. Because you chose to enter physical life, we honor you. Now, act from your greatness. Be confident that you are important. Live a sovereign life. Amen.

KNOW OF THE COMING OF PEACE

The greatest time and the greatest energy are becoming available now. Greatness is opening now. Many of you know this already. Many of you can't see this possibility, and many more never will see the greatness coming to life. Nevertheless, the good news is that there is an awakening. Earth is opening to a new way of being. As we have said, this will take time to unfold, and the time is beginning now. Babies will be born into a loving world. Children will grow up loving and respecting themselves and others. We are happy to announce the coming of peace. No matter what your situation is now, in your heart, it is time to tune into peace. It is time to accept that it is present and everyone can begin to enjoy. As you begin to open to the idea of peace, you will be contributing to the energy of peace. As you become aware, so will others. The time is now for the awareness of a coming peace. If you contribute for a moment, an hour, or a day, your contribution will help magnificently. Your world will change because of millions of moments of peaceful thought by millions of people. Accept this with gratitude. Let It Be.

THE KEEPER OF PEACE

This is a good day to talk about spreading the word and sharing the emotions of love. Today is about peace. How about starting an international peace day? Put it on your calendar to celebrate international peace. Make it a day to end fighting and harsh words. Make it a day to say something nice even to those you don't like. Especially reach out to those in prisons. The guards and the prisoners could all use a kind word and a sign of peace. This is a dream, and only you in physical form can make it a reality. You are the keeper of peace. Imagine it. International Peace Day.

And now, more about peacekeeping. What would you rather be, a peacekeeper or a peacemaker? In the beginning, there was a peace maker. There still is. The peacemaker lives within all of you, and you all have become the peacekeepers. Every life form is a peacekeeper. Every life form can choose to develop this ability or to discount the peace within. We think it is nice that you have the power of peace. Share it with each other.

FOREVERLAND

Today we are excited to talk about leveraging and equalizing Earth and the universe. This is exciting stuff. Now that you all have been told that people on Earth are a part of the larger picture it is time to understand the whole of all. It is a good time to understand the whole of this great, magnificent, large and infinite foreverland- home to all- not just you on Earth. There is a flow. There is an energy flow which goes through it all. This flow is affected by your energy flow. That is to say that all the energy around you can be affected by your energy. That also means that you are more than just a physical body in a physical place. You are a contributor to the whole of all that is. We find that to be exciting and we hope you do too.

In forever land, your existence is infinite although your mass form will change.

BEAUTY

Welcome back to another beautiful day inside and out. The beauty of the day is what we want you to look at. This will be easier to do if all is well within you, and flowers are blooming etc. This can also be easy even if you are not happy. If you are sad or angry, it can still be a beautiful day for you. That is because the beauty is always present; it is your awareness that might need to change. The good news is that you have power over your awareness, your attitudes, and your feelings. The control is within you. We suggest looking through a different perspective. It doesn't matter what your event of the day may be. What matters most is the way you choose to view the day. At least see the beauty once in a while each day then comment on the beauty to others. That will help them to see the beauty also. Laugh once in a while every day. It is your choice and your purpose. The beauty comes from within.

PEACE IN TOGETHERNESS

We are ready to continue our talks of togetherness. The only way that planet Earth will survive is by joining together in peace. This is about everyone. It isn't about your leaders or the winner of your wars; it is about recognition of peace and love in the hearts (spirit) of everyone. Put in your mind that it isn't about your-way-or-no-way. Togetherness and peace are about experiencing eternal love within. It is about God, love, source, whole, HEF- high frequency energy, being experienced within everyone. The continuation of life on Earth isn't about a particular man-inspired religion or philosophy. It is about accepting infinite love. One law, one truth. Now isn't that simple? One energy connects you all. That is where you will find togetherness in peace.

The struggle to find self begins with letting go of "them." You can't give to them unless you first experience what you want to give- in you.

I'm talking about confidence and believing in you. It helps knowing that you are a part of the greatest. You are an extension of love. In times of doubt, get quiet and tune in to the god within. Believe in your greater good. Believe that all is right from the place within. Come together with your inner self, your spirit, your connection to all that is. Come together with "you" so that you can come together with "them."

A FUN BREAK FROM THE STRUGGLE

Now, let's have some fun. It might be time to get up and shake off the dreariness. Get up, put on a bit of happy music, and move with the rhythm. Now, is a good time to express joy and happiness- even if only for a minute. Know that all is well on the larger scale. Be aware that your present situation will change. We suggest you change right now to happiness. And hold it, hold it, hold it, as long as you can. Happiness is healthiness.

Now that you have had your fun break, your happy break, we will talk more about struggling to overcome negative energy. The best way is to give up the struggle. Surrender the struggle. Peace will come when there is an opening in the struggle. The obvious question then is how to give up the struggle. The answer is to focus elsewhere. Train yourself. Work at it until refocusing becomes natural. In the beginning, your tendency will be to hold on to your negative energy about the perceived negative event. Maybe you don't even want to let it go. You've probably been well trained to hold on to the negative energy. We suggest that you practice letting go for as long as you can. When negative energy returns, practice again, and again. There is plenty of positive energy to focus on. No excuses there. Become aware of your energy. Focus on the good stuff.

STRUGGLES AND JOY IN FOREVERLAND

We will talk about the struggles and the Joy in Foreverland. Your home. Do you want to know what the best part is? The best part is that you will always be here, one way or another, and joy will always be here, in one form or another. The struggles are mostly optional.

Now let's get on with business. You see, you are energy. Everything is energy. Energy will never cease to be. You have the ability to create movement with energy. Because you are in physical form, you have a greater ability to create and move positive energy and negative energy. When you struggle, it is usually about negative energy that you are involved with. To stop the struggle, switch over to positive energy. Yes, yes, you can. Practice. Until you get better at it, at least switch over to… shall we say a flat energy. A holding place until you can reach that higher place. Put all your fears, hates, depressions, etc., on hold until you can experience more clarity and more relief. Refuse to allow the negative emotions/energy as much as you can. Release them, let go. We know that this can take time. Start working on it.

The joy is waiting for you. Believe that if you let go of negative energy, positive energy will fill its place. Allow. Repeat as necessary. Become what you want to experience. Become love. Become joy. Now is a good time to start the process. It is a process. It is the process of learning love, learning a new world of peace for you and for all. Take your time to develop the process, but start now to enjoy forever. We love you.

TRUTHS AND FACTS

Today, a new day is a good day to look at truths. The truth is that this is a decision time for your future. The truth is that your kids and grandchildren will inherit a thriving planet or a destroyed planet. This isn't a science fiction story. It is a fact about your home. The best way to keep home on Earth is to become aware of direction. Fact, Now Is The Time to choose a path. Either you join together or lose to destruction. Someone somewhere will lead towards peace, while someone somewhere will lead towards destruction. Let me say that everyone will follow according to their heart- spirit- or the absence thereof. That means from the love within- the desire to join, to negotiate, to accept differences or to react out of fear, hate, judgments. This is true not only for each other but for the planet itself. The equations are simple, high energy frequencies = love = life, while low energy frequencies = fear = death. Those are facts. The truth is that you can choose to become aware of where you will lead and who you will follow. Will it be towards walls, boundaries, divisions, and separation, or openness, freedom and oneness?

Now, we will let you know that drawing a line to separate will not accomplish peace. Any time that you separate you from another or from a group, a country, or a continent will not bring peace. Do you get it? Do you understand that separation is devastation? It is through the connection you all have, to the whole of all that is, that you all will find the answers. It is through connection, not separation. Connection to the whole, the source, the god, the energy of forever will connect you all to each other mentally and spiritually. Your roots are the same.

MANIFESTING, CREATING, AND MOVING POSITIVE ENERGY

Moving on it is time to talk more about the importance of life- manifesting, creating, being one with all there is. Your role, your purpose is to create and move positive energy. Of course, you can't create energy, but you can change energy. By doing so, you create more positive and less negative. And that is your purpose. The more you create the better your planet... and forever land will be. The better also means the happier, more joyful, less troubled, less conflicted life you will lead. As a matter of fact, you can live this life NOW, even if the whole of Earth is not living it with you. We invited you to be different. We invite you to live as if you have it all- because you do. Have it in spirit so that it can manifest in your physical world. Know that first the peace, joy, love comes from within. Next, it is manifested into your physical life. No matter what you are creating, it starts from within. Create positive energy. Create joy. Create love. Amen.

THE MESSAGES OF THE TEACHERS

We want to tell you about the messages of the teachers. You see, the teachers have been around for many centuries. Just like you, they are a part of the whole of all that is. Just like you, they have lived in physical form. Presently they are in spiritual form. The teachers have learned to incorporate the words they bring to you. They learned to live by the words as a truth. By sharing the words, they want everyone to understand then incorporate the messages. That means to believe, to love, to live the truth of the words. It is one thing to read the words, quite another to live them... to be the words. As we have said, this can come with practice. It will take some time to let go of the old ways and make space for the new. The time to begin is today. Maybe start with one section. One truth. Build from there. We will be here to help and guide. You are never alone.

REDEEMING YOUR VALUE

And now we will continue. It is time to talk about redemption. Redeeming the value of your service. It is with much gratitude that we see and acknowledge your strengths and your suffering while on Earth in physical form. Do you understand that while in spiritual form, you chose to re-enter the physical realm? For many and various reasons, the spirit re-enters the physical. The goal is always to move energy into a positive place. Always. For whatever reason you have come back into physical form, we want you to know that you are appreciated and loved. No matter what you do while in physical form, you are loved. Begin thinking about your loving self. Begin living from your loving self. Begin experiencing your loving self. Beyond a doubt, beyond all hatred, is your loving self. Get to know it.

JUSTIFICATION

The need to justify, make sense, or explain your behavior... the things you do. Rationalize to create acceptance and harmony with your conscious, unconscious, physical, and spiritual self. Not necessarily only to others, but to yourself. This needs to be done only when your thoughts and actions are out of sync with your loving self. You see, behaving in an unloving-of-self way creates friction within. To reduce friction, make excuses that seem justifiable. Believable. Realistic. Usually people don't even realize that they are doing this. Usually, this comes from subconscious programing. Usually the programming began in defense of self while being unlovingly attacked by someone else. Let me simplify. You learned how to make bad things feel better. You got used to it, and eventually made bad things feel better without even thinking about it. It is time to think about it. Now is the time to think about and bring awareness to acting from your unloving self. Acting from your unloving self is acting from your fearful self. There was a time when it was important to act from your fearful self. The time has passed.

Now is the time to act from your loving self. Remove the dissonance between your brain and your heart, your conscious and your unconscious, your spiritual and physical self. Remove the fear by getting to know and trust your loving self- your connection to the greater whole of all that exists. Honestly, you can't go wrong when you are connected to the greatest, strongest, most powerful energy of all. In the short-term, it may seem easier to justify. In the long term you are an infinite self. Go for the big picture. Live large. Live from the greatest power of all- and find peace with all the parts of yourself. No need to justify.

STRENGTH IN TIME OF NEED

Just for the sake of knowing, we will talk about gathering your strength in time of need. In time of need means anytime you are living from a place other than your loving self. When you are living from your fearful place and experiencing something like fear, hate, anger, sadness... you might need some strength to get back to your loving self. The number one rule we can tell you is that these feelings do not come from an event in your life. They come from inside you. Therefore the feelings are fixable by you. The event does not have to get better in order for you to feel better. Let's imagine that you or your precious loved one is near death and you are sad, angry, etc. This is probably a good time to find extra strength. If you can't change the circumstance, then change your perspective. Experience love for your dying self or dying loved one. Feel the love within. Experience gratitude for all the experiences that you or your loved one had. Find strength in love and gratitude. You won't find it in fear, anger, sadness. Create joy within your dying self. Laugh a bit. It will give you strength. The same is true for any circumstance that you are separating from. Money, marriage... whatever is giving you sorrow is based in fear. You have the strength internally to get through. Gather strength through the higher frequencies. That is where you will be sustained during the rough times. It is your choice, your frequencies. Use whatever gives you strength when you need it.

YOUR ENDLESS TIME

Do you want to know about the time and the present? Are you ever interested in now? Time is a revolving, ever moving sequence of events. It is linear in relationship to your physical existence on Earth. It is fluid in your relationship in the spiritual. We tell you this to hopefully reduce stress. You see, in the spiritual picture, time cannot be a stressor. Time is never ending never beginning. Time is anywhere you want to be with just a desire. So much easier. Now, to make it easier for the physical world, know that your beginning and end is a quick glance into anywhere. That is to say that from the spirit world, you can be seen in the past and the present and the future. You are endless. We say this to help you realize that the life you are in right now can be treated as a joyful adventure in forever if you want it to be. Someday you may look back or forward at this time in body. Will you see stress and worry, or a happy physical person? Your choice. Doesn't really matter. Just letting you know that it is nothing to stress over. We are hoping that you will go ahead and have fun while spreading positive energy. See you around.

RUMBLINGS, CLASHES, AND PEACE

We want to share the news of a coming event. The event is peace on earth. It really isn't just a single event. It is more of a gradual growth of positive energy until the end result is peace on Earth. Exciting stuff. All the people on Earth will eventually participate. Right now, there are big shake-ups which create awareness. Rumbles in human behavior both positive and negative are creating a stir of awakenings. Be assured that the rumblings are necessary. Know that it is a sign of necessary change. The conflicts and clashes will bring awareness and wake-up calls to those who would otherwise not recognize the need for change. Now is the time for awareness of changing times that will lead to peace. We say this to help you look at the clashes without a lot of fear and predictions of doom. It is much better that you all look forward to the creation of peace. The outcome of the rumblings and clashes will be a unity of peace.

Together again. The world will come together again in peace. Each and every one of you is participating in one way or another. Whether or not you realize it, you are all accepting or opposing the movement towards peace. A lot of positions will have to be given up. A lot of equalizing will happen. The good news is that the movement is in order and changes are happening. That is to say, energy frequencies will change. Negative frequencies will decline- but not without a struggle. And that is what you will see, the stirring of negative energy. You will also begin to see the resolution, positive energy- the peaceful movement. Let it be.

GRAVITY

Now let's talk about gravity- something that most of you take for granted. Gravity is your word for the glue that binds, the glue that holds Earth life together. In our view, Gravity is an energy field. As we have said, energy is both positive and negative. You can probably imagine that the energy, the gravity around Earth is positive, negative... and neutral. You, the people on Earth have some control over this gravity energy field. Not total control, but let's say that you have an influence. Doesn't that make sense? Can you see that all energy affects all energy? The stone tossed in the pond ripples all the water. If you can accept this, then you can probably speculate that your use of energy on Earth affects gravity. That is to say that the way you treat the planet, and each other, affects more than just the physical boundaries that you can touch. The way you move energy on Earth affects more than the top of the mountain or the bottom of the sea. Your energy reaches into space and into the glue that binds. Your gravity is also affected as your energy expands outward. We recommend conscious awareness of your power. It is a good time to become aware of industry and productivity. Become aware of what you consume. There is more than enough of what is needed to sustain all life on Earth. The negative energy of greed isn't necessary.

Let's go for the punch, the gusto. Let's go for an extreme rationale. Let's go for truth. No fluff, just the facts. The truth is that The Time Is Now to move forward into a productive pattern. Truth, positive energy sustains life. Truth, negative energy destroys life. Have I made myself clear? Good. Now it is your turn to make decisions about the type of energy you generate. Even if you're very comfortably generating abundance for yourself but lack for others, it's time to think about it in a broader perspective. Wake up. Become conscious of the energy you are creating for planet Earth.

RICHNESS AND ABUNDANCE FOR ALL

It is time to start feeling the richness. Create a mindset of abundance. No one is lacking. That is to say that everyone is equally connected to an abundant world. Everyone can believe in their own wealth. We hope that everyone will begin to believe in their connection to all that is, which includes abundance. The sooner everyone believes the sooner greed and poverty will end.

Let's look at some scenarios; the child born into a physically wealthy and educated family versus the child born into poverty and ignorance. Both children are equally connected to the energy of abundance. Both children are equally connected to the energy of love/life. Both children are equal in spirit. Look at the child born to experience physical health, attractiveness, and strength. Look at the child born to experience physical illness, crippling, and minimum strength. In the spirit world, they are equal. Their physical differences are not an entitlement to abundance. Prosperity is a gift for everyone. There is enough for everyone. It is old, worn out, and nonfunctional beliefs that created the separation. Now is the time for everyone to grow a physical existence which includes all of life on Earth. Now is the time to end competition for survival. Now is the time. Reach out to each other knowing there is enough. Ponder the possibility of enough for everyone. Think about it. Let the energy begin to swirl in your thoughts. The seeds of equality and richness will be planted.

WITH YOU THROUGH THE CHANGE

We are ready to write about the time of change and what it will look like. Gone will be the empires built at the cost of low paid laborers. That is good news and worth celebrating. Also, gone will be wars fought over possessions- land, lovers, goods.... In the new world, there will be unity, not separation. Beliefs will be for the betterment of all. Beliefs will be for the betterment of Earth. We agree that this will take time and it will be time well spent. We also know that the seeds are being planted NOW. We know that many people can see this vision and more people are joining regularly. It really isn't so difficult to visualize. Once the vision becomes present, doubt will begin to decline. New beliefs will start forming. You can say that the seed would have been planted.

To be sure, the process won't be all easy. As we have said, some will see the vision; others will fight the vision, while still others will not wake up to the vision within their lifetime. It is all expected. The differences will present clashes. The clashes are evidence of changing times. We suggest that you hold on to the big picture of inevitable peace. The peace will be in your heart, in your spirit. We suggest that you avoid the drama as much as possible by staying connected to your inner strength. Your inner strength contains the highest, most powerful energy available. Your inner strength is love. We appreciate you. We support you. We will be with you through it all.

With love,

The Teachers and Guides

BEGIN TO MOVE THE MOUNTAIN

Today we will talk about moving mountains. We mean mountains of energy not rocks. It is imperative that negative energy is decreased while positive energy is increased. Adjustments will be made in your thinking, believing, and acting. One pebble, one rock at a time, begin the process of noticing your energy- your feelings. Start by noticing. Play around with it. Change your energy. You have the power. This isn't about the events in your life. Events come and go. You have a stronger power than the earthly events. With practice, you will realize that feelings and events can be separated. Practice adding joy to your sad times- or practice adding sadness to your joyful times. The process works either way and you have the control switch. In time, this will become easy. When it does, your world view will change. The drama in your life will disappear. Sickness will decline and health will be on the rise. This is a fact. With better health comes more joy. A higher awareness of your energy will change the world… if you allow. Start with a pebble of thought energy, a pebble of belief.

PART TWO

N ow it is time to practice some of the changes. Now is the time to work in the direction of peace for all on Earth. By doing so I mean that you can actively make a change by making a choice.

YOUR CONTRIBUTION TO PHYSICAL CHANGE
We are ready to begin talking about making physical changes. Creating physical change is what you can do while in a physical body. You were not able to create physical change while you were in spiritual form so you made the decision to re-enter the physical world. For whatever reason you chose, you are here in physical form to create physical change. Know that while you are here, you are still, and always will be, connected to the whole of all that is. You still have the power to create change using your connection to the highest energy frequencies, the highest power. We suggest that you tune in regularly. We will help guide each person. It is our joy, our pleasure to guide.

CHANGES
The changes which will occur will benefit all life and planet Earth. We want you all to recognize and know that wealth is associated with having abundance. You all have abundance so there is no need to hoard, fight, or kill for wealth. There is a need to change perspective. Let go of he/she has- I have not position even if that is your experience.

A better position for everyone is the knowledge that there is enough, the planet is plentiful; no one has to be excluded. Everyone is born entitled. Doesn't that sound joyful? Isn't that something you would want to breathe into and accept?

An action plan is to redefine greed. We define it as fear which creates the need to hoard. It is a false security. True security and abundance comes from the use of positive energy- the more, the better. Change your beliefs and create abundance for all. It will happen with or without you. The difference is that it will happen sooner with your participation.

Our first goal as guides of action is to instill in you the desire to equalize this abundant planet Earth. It is a fact that 'I have – you don't have' will not bring peace. The idea that everyone has is an idea that everyone can live with peacefully. Now, the first thing to do is to acknowledge that there is enough and that everyone is born into equal shares of abundance. When you know this, accept this, and believe this law, changes will begin.

THE CONSEQUENCES AND THE ACTION

Next, we will tell you that the time is near for choosing togetherness and peace. The time is now to start considering the consequences of your actions, consequences to all of Earth. Consider your thoughts and actions. Plan on reaping what is sowed. With that said, we are speaking of the consequence of life on Earth. Each and every person plays a role and must choose a position of either positive energy of love, joy, happiness or negative energy of fear which equals greed, hunger, death etc. It can be no other way. Some of you feel insignificant as if your thoughts don't matter to the big picture of Earth. I guarantee that you do matter to the whole of Earth. In the final say, it will be the everyday people, not the presumed bosses or leaders who will change the energy of Earth. The everyday common people will take a stance which will lead us into togetherness or will lead us into separation. For now, know that each of you are important and each of you are loved. We want you to make decisions that are good for the whole. We will help you to know the good of the whole. We will teach and guide. Information will be available. For now, believe in your loving self. We do. We believe in the love within you.

Now is the time to wake up to a new direction of peace. The dawning is here with the excitement of a better world. Now let's talk about what this will look like. What we see you can imagine. What we see is a brighter glow around the planet. The brighter glow comes with higher levels of energy frequencies. In translation, that means a more loving planet with more loving people using the most powerful and longest reaching waves of energy. Can you imagine? On your level, you will probably see fewer prisons, fewer wars, less hunger, less disease... You will see more smiles, more hugs, more friendships. Your experience will be peacefulness, playfulness, and joy, in your work, community, and your home. Greed will turn into sharing, anger will turn into understanding. Are you getting the picture? Good, and you can create this world. Everyone will participate. This is what the great leaders of the world have been saying to you all along- for thousands of years. Now is the time to take action. Believe in your loving self. That is an action.

THE ACTION PLAN
The plan is to rethink. The plan is to become aware. Then the plan is to create an action that alters the course. Again, from our position we recognize your desire to survive comfortably while in physical form. This isn't in conflict with our desire for you. This isn't in conflict with raising positive energy for Earth. The conflict is with each individual working against each other. The conflict is one person creating negative energy towards another person... and on it goes. The solution to the conflict is to create positive energy for you and for others. Simple. The problem is, once again, fear. Fear that if one person has, the other person has not. Fear of giving to one will cause depletion in the giver. There is abundance for all. It is not possible to run out of positive energy. Positive energy is the micro level of physical abundance. Can you understand on a scientific level that physical goods come

from positive energy? We see how this can be difficult to understand when "good" people often experience less than 'bad' people. Let me be clear in saying that abundance is not about good or bad people. It is about positive or negative energy directed.

Now, let's move on in the direction of peace. The direction is clear. The purpose is clear. Moving positive energy creates peace. As we have said, the purpose of being in physical form is to move energy. It is time for the people of Earth to move less negative energy and more positive energy. That is the action. That is the plan. Where to begin? Begin in your heart- your spirituality. Begin observing and noticing what you say, think, and do. Notice if you feel joyful or irritable. Notice if you go through most days happily or sad. Notice if you see the positive or the negative in yourself and in the other person. If you see the positive, smile and say thanks to yourself for seeing what you want to see. If you see negative, change it. Don't question, challenge, or try to explain- just change it. Change the negative to a positive then give thanks to yourself for seeing the brighter side of life.

This is an opportunity to love your enemy. It isn't necessary to physically hug your enemy. What we are saying is change your negative energy of bad feelings toward someone you don't like to a positive energy. This isn't about the other person being what you would consider good or bad. No, this is about you and how you think, see, and act towards the other person. It is you whom we invite to change. We invite you to view others through the eyes of your spiritual self. Practice. This skill may take time to develop. If you struggle with changing your negative energy to positive energy, then practice going neutral until you can get to positive. Complement yourself each step of the way. Giving yourself gratitude helps cement the process. Self-gratitude helps you to feel better. When you feel better, you experience the "better" all around. Practice.

MORE ACTION
Let's rev it up a bit and take the action of going out of your way into the way of peace. Take a step in that direction. Take a step into creating

and offering a kindness. Do it not because we said so, but because your spiritual self says so. Further the action by acknowledging that you listened to your spiritual self. Your brain and your heart communicated. Your physical and your spiritual communicated. Praise yourself. That is an action.

GO FOR THE GUSTO

You have everything to win by going all out in the peace movement for all of Earth. This is about winners, not about losers and winners. What you have now are winners and losers. It isn't fun for all. We want everyone to win. And everyone can win because everyone is a particle of infinite love, infinite life. Everyone. Pick up your feet and start dancing to the music of life. Everyone is invited to share in fun, joy, happiness, and love. Do you know that the first step is the most exciting? What we are saying is get up and own your value. Get up and know your worth. Get up and celebrate *YOU* while you can. While you are here on Earth in physical form, make your visit worthwhile. Promoting yourself sends positive light energy into space. You are worth it. Your light will radiate forever. Now get up and get on with the gusto of living. And while you are at it, send radiance to others. Don't be shy about to whom you send radiant joy. Just feel the joy and it will transmit.

DEVELOP RICHNESS

Now Is The Time to discover the inner wealth that you possess. If you want your physical wealth to manifest, let it first manifest inside in spirit. You see, that is how it works. Experience all the wealth within you. It is limitless. Know that you have everything in spirit. Know that you are connected to all that is. Know that you can create in the physical world by first creating in the spiritual world. What you would really be doing is moving your personal physical energy at an unseen level. The energy you work with is the energy that will be used to develop your physical goods. Everyone has this power. You may have only known poverty and have no understanding of how to escape. We tell you, recognize your richness by knowing that you are connected to everything. This will probably take some time to believe and manifest. Start now. Each step of the way, show appreciation and gratitude. By doing so, you are saying yes, I want more of what I'm getting. We are saying to feel joy, feel love, feel happiness knowing that you have the power to create goodness. You are not a victim of your circumstances unless you think you are. No matter how down you may feel, you still have a light inside that connects you to the greatest light of love-god-life-infinity-the whole of all that is. Your connection will take you the same distance as anyone else. No one was singled out to suffer. No one. Everyone is singled out to thrive. Do you get that? We hope so because when everyone begins to understand, the energy of richness and poverty will shift. Those who figure it out, can help the others to understand. Help or hinder each other according to your love or greed. Your choice. Know that now is the time to develop richness in yourself and in others. Begin.

DISCOVERING YOUR BELIEFS
It may be a good idea to break your beliefs down into knowable parts. Starting with the obvious, you are aware of being alive and in physical form. You are aware that people pass out of physical form. You might have a problem believing in what you can't see. Those who can see, communicate, have intuition, etc., can believe in life separate from the physical body. For those of you who can't, begin discovering the source of your beliefs. Possibly you were taught a particular belief and stuck with it unquestioningly. Some of you don't know what to believe so consciously don't bother to think about your beliefs. We want you to know that wherever your beliefs may be, the truth lies within each and every one of you. And that is a good place for discovery of your beliefs. Once you begin to question, answers will begin to arrive. The answers have always been present, just waiting for your readiness to receive.

We are inviting you to discover more of who you are. This will take time. It's a journey worth taking. Discover inside of you, a belief in infinite truth. Once you discover, you will believe, once you believe, peace will be with you and all of Earth. This is an action- get to know the source of your beliefs.

HEARING WITHOUT EARS

We want to talk about listening. If you think about how you hear, you will probably say that a noise out there went in through my ears and I could hear. You might say that deafness prevents hearing. We want to say that sound is energy waves. Even though you can't see them, they exist. Everything moves on waves of energy. We want to say that deafness- a physical malfunction in the ear, does not prevent hearing. Communication happens with or without sound because there are many waves of communication- that are not visible. Those who don't hear with their ears, usually have increased abilities in other forms of sensory awareness. We want you to know that each of you has the ability to hear without sound. Listening can be done by knowing. The knowing is done by listening on the frequency of your connection to god, infinite source... Everyone does this. Some people are occasionally aware, some are not. Prayer and meditation are ways of communicating without ears. Some people have wakened in the middle of the night *knowing* that a loved one had died. Others *hear* a message from someone who is miles away, or deceased. There are ways of hearing without ears. Hear on the energy wavelengths of infinite source. Quite a chatter box it can be. Tune in any time.

YOUR ENERGY EMISSIONS

Now we will talk about the comings and goings of infinite space. You see, Earth is a part of the whole picture. You, as a part of life on Earth, energize the planet, which energizes the universe and beyond. It is a system which links everything together. It shouldn't come as a surprise that all is linked and that what happens on Earth will affect areas outside of Earth. Just as the sun affects our temperatures and the moon affects our waters Earth's energy is felt outside of our planet. The types of energy frequencies you use have long reaching effects. Become conscious of your energy frequencies... emotions that you emit. You probably wouldn't like it if the sun got angry and decided not to shine. OK, not possible but we think it helps you to understand. The point is that you are important and you matter to this infinite place. Become aware of the energy you emit. Practice emitting the good stuff. The world thanks you.

HEALING FROM THE DESTRUCTION ON EARTH

With love, there is life. They are synonymous. Life grows. That means Earth can and will heal from its scars once the destruction stops. Presently, the light energy surrounding Earth has dim spots, and less bright light along with the long rays of brightness. No one wants the lights to dim, fade, or go out. The desire for Earth is brilliance- long reaching bright, brilliant frequencies of energy. Pay attention to what is happening with Earth, the physical land and waters, and the life of plants, and animals- which includes humans. Pay attention to what is thriving and what is disappearing. Pay attention to the love of Earth. Pay attention to the life you all share. We ask that rules of everlasting life be foremost in every action plan. We ask that you consider the result of your plans for progress. Is it short term or long term? Is the progress for all of Earth? Focus on what is being destroyed in order to move forward. Weigh the costs. You, the plan maker, will someday leave physical earth physical body. Plan on leaving it in better condition than when you arrived with your plan. Plan on brightness for all. Plan on life/love in your business plan. Yes, Earth will heal. The time is now to plan.

THE ACTION PLAN OF ABUNDANCE

We are ready to talk about prosperity. To prosper is to live abundantly, to have that which you desire. Prosperity is a seed of joy. Yes, joy. It isn't expected for people to live in poverty. It isn't necessary. In order to attain joy through prosperity, plant the seed. The seeds of prosperity are plentiful, everlasting, and always available. The choice to plant the seed is yours. What we are saying is to envision your wealth. Experience it as a spiritual truth. Know that spiritually you are wealthy. That is the beginning- the seed. Know this. The knowing of spiritual wealth will overflow into physical wealth. This isn't about you being good or bad. It is believing that you are *entitled* to draw from all that is. You are entitled to draw from the infinite energy of all that is. The sooner you believe and act, the sooner you will witness prosperity. And as you begin to witness, be sure to express gratitude. Notice what you are receiving, not what you don't have, then be grateful. Do you understand? You are spiritually, abundantly connected to the energy of life. Plant that seed in your mind. Observe the physical development of prosperity. Give thanks. That is the action plan of abundance.

FOREVER TIME, INFINITE TIME

Do you want to know about forever time? Do you ever wonder about infinite time? You are a part of it, and always will be. Right now, right where you are, you are connected with always. You might as well begin to live joyfully and lovingly- your purpose while in physical form. Your energy is forever and will never die. It is your life force. Everyone you know is also connected to infinite time. *You* are the god within. Because you are a part of "god" and infinite source, you have much more power to create than you've probably imagined. Within you is the power you pray to, meditate to, and long for in times of need. Does that change your game plan? We hope so. We hope it is enlightening to know your power. Your connection to all is within. Once you know, believe, and understand this truth, you will be able to act differently. Maybe you will act with more confidence. Maybe you will continue communication with prayer, idle thoughts, or meditation. Just know that the prayer line is closer than your might have thought. That is all for now. Spend some time thinking about it. After all, you have forever time to think this through.

MORE BRIGHT IDEAS

We have more bright ideas for you; ideas which can help you create a stronger glow of light. We think it would be nice for you all to experience the light within, the glow of love. For those of you who are consciously aware of your light within, we suggest that you use it frequently. You can do this by smiling more often, hugging, being a bit silly whenever possible, singing and dancing for the fun of it. In other words, spend more time in high frequency energy activities. Express your glow often.

For those of you who don't experience the light within, we want to help you. Everyone has the right to this experience. For those of you who squash the light in others, we want to help you too. We want you all to know that YOU are a part of a loving world. You can know this because love = life. You are alive therefore love is a part of your makeup. Every physical form is connected to a life loving spiritual self. Every human, animal, plant, and planet is connected. This is a truth. Come to know this truth. Come to know and believe in the truth that you are in physical form because spiritual love/life is within you. When you exit physical form and the physical body decomposes, your spiritual love will continue, thrive, and glow forever. We suggest that you allow your physical form and the physical form of others to experience this glowing life force. That is your purpose. Your purpose is to glow and continue the life force. Your purpose is to use your physical body in high frequency, light energy waves. Get used to it. That is our bright idea.

FOREVER MORE MY LOVE
In infinite time love goes on, and on, and on. Forever. Get used to it. Experience infinite love. We want you to know this so that some of the bickering and sadness will end. We want you to know that your love for another will go on forever even if you physically separate in the present life time. Isn't that good to know? The reason is, your physical loving connection to another comes from infinite love. All love is infinite. Physical love for another passes, but not the infinite connection. You may have many loves within a physical life time. Loves can last for fleeting moments or for many years. The truth is, love is that connection to infinite, not to another physical form. Physical love is a reverberation of infinite love. We suggest that you don't grieve the coming and

going, and don't try to hoard or be jealous. Accept a loving relationship for what it is then let go. Know that the love you felt is stored in infinite time. The physical body that the love was directed towards will leave. It must. The love you expressed or felt is forever. Rest assured.

Now, with this knowledge, give and receive love freely and often. Express love not fear. The fear is about your belief of being alone and lonely without love. Not spiritually possible. In infinite time you are always loved, and never alone. The love you create will last forever. We understand the times of not having a physical love. Do you understand that the love you are sharing with another is coming from and endless infinite supply? Give freely, receive freely. There is nothing to fight over. Love is forever, with or without a body.

A TIME OF CELEBRATION

Let's start in the beginning again. You see, there was a time when love was not as important as physical survival. We can call it an emotionless time or a time without much feeling.

The world has evolved. Life forms have learned to connect to deeper meaning. Life forms learned to feel energy frequencies. They learned to tune in. You can almost say that they learned to manipulate energy through feelings. That is good news. Now Is The Time to manipulate energy towards the light- towards high energies. As we have said, high energy frequencies maintain life. We want you all to know that this is a purpose. You are in body to produce high frequencies of life energy. You have evolved. Planet Earth has evolved. It is a good time, to celebrate. Celebrate life on Earth evolving to the level of energy awareness and manipulation. Now celebrate an awakening to high frequency energy. Just to be sure you understand, celebrate joy, love, peace, and happiness. Celebrate continued life. Love is life.

Just in case you missed the understanding, Earth survived. Earth survived to the level of mass devastation or mass peace. Know that *now* is a time of new direction. The river will bend towards the fork of peace or the fork of destruction. Now is the time to choose and take action.

REASONING AND INSTINCTS

Now, let's get on with the developing stories. You see, once upon a time, long ago, people did not reason. Neither did most types of animals. They reacted. The reactions were based on instincts. This was before the time of reason, before development of the ability to think things through. This instinct was dominant for action. Now, both instinct and reason exist in humans. Old ideas of kill-first-think-later still exist but those traits will be dying off in generations to come. For now, the time is of awareness. The time is of becoming aware of reason. Instinct will change following awareness. The new instinct will be towards survival of all. This will come following awareness. Think of it like learning to walk. The toddler has to be aware of a desire to walk, and then be aware of taking steps before walking becomes a new ability. The same is true with learning most new ways of being. There is an old instinctive way of being, an awakened way of being, and a new instinctive way of being. Wake up to a new level of reasoning. The ability exists to reason with new enlightenment. New reasoning will create new instinctive ways of being. Wake up. Love is the new way.

BIRTHING INFINITE LOVE

We want to talk about birthing a new way of being. The seed was planted. The awareness is developing. Actions are already being taken for generating a love based planet Earth. An Earth that survives. Survival means less death, destruction, disease, etc. The key to survival is infinite love. That is the only way. The only way is through attaching to the whole of all- the god, the whole, the source, the HEF-high energy frequencies. It is a fact that Earth cannot be maintained in isolation from the energy that feeds all. It is a fact that both positive and negative energy exists now on planet Earth. It is a fact that humans hold the power to create more positive or more negative energy. This is a fact of life or death. Become aware. Wake up to your choices. Understand the truth of isolation-separation and the truth of oneness. Isolate from each other and the source of all, or join in with each other and the source of all. Do this for yourself and your planet. We believe many of you understand. We believe many more will become understanding. The name of this birthing is Infinite Love on Earth.

RE-CREATING FROM INFINITE LOVE

Now is the time to re-create. Create from a place of infinite love. You can never go wrong with this kind of creating. Realistically, it is time to act from a place of infinite love. We understand that many people don't understand infinite love and don't recognize having experienced it. First, believe that loving another person or life form is limiting when compared to infinite love. Physical love is a good thing. Just know that there is more and seek to experience the *more* which is available to you. The seeking will guide you. Know that the experience of seeking will sharpen awareness. When you become aware of the feeling, the experience, be grateful. Joy will help lead you and so will peace. A joyful and peaceful way of being separate from physical events will get you closer. For no reason, seek the experience of joy, and the state of peacefulness. Next, seek the experience of love from within. Seek non-directed love. Not directed towards another, but to feel the experience within. Practice. On an ordinary day, in your ordinary physical life, seek an inner connection. Re-create from your highest, strongest, most powerful self. Re-create from your power of infinite love.

THE ANSWER TO THE END OF SEPARATION

Let's talk about the end and the answers, the end of separation between your brain and your spirit. They aren't really separate but often people use them separately which is often the problem. It is time to convene on a different platform. The time is now to face the dawning of a new way of being. It is time.

The wheels of change are turning, the path is laid out and being paved with voices of reason. There is a multitude of people who understand the change and are acting on its behalf. One by one, others will join. We want you to be aware of the changes for planet Earth. Be aware that voices are rising to separate the truth from the greed, the light from the dark. Truth- there is enough for everyone, and everyone can live peacefully. Greed will spoil the Earth, fight against wholeness, and create destruction. The light, the awareness, the peace and love will protect you and Earth. The dark, negative energy will destroy. Is that clear enough? Do you understand? The choice belongs to everyone. The answers will come from within you. Listen inside, ask inside. Know from your spirit within, which is connected to the big picture of all that is. None of you need to act like sheep letting others lead. Everyone has equal connection to the truth. The truth will guide you. When I say *the truth*, know for sure that the truth is found by listening through your spiritual self, not your physical brain. Feel the truth, feel the untruth, then make a choice. The truth feels peaceful, the untruth feels guilty. There, that is the answer.

THE TIMING IS NOW TO BEGIN REJOICING
And now, it is time to look at the path of love, life, and success for all. On this path we see advancement of a planet. We see a brighter light on and around your planet. We are pleased to announce a movement in this direction. We are pleased to say that eventually, EVERYONE will join to create heaven on Earth. We know it is possible and we know that, in your spirit, there is willingness. We smile as your love begins to radiate from you, and above you. We praise each and every one of you for your participation. The truth is that you are breaking through with ultimate glory. Let it be known that the world is changing. Talk about this with optimism. Speak with hope and joy. The uprising is planned. The timing is now. Rejoice.

Now that you are in the spirit of rejoicing, take the next step and celebrate life- all of life. The celebration begins with openness and acceptance of all life. You see, you are like a snowflake in the iceberg, a grain of sand in the dessert. Celebrate you and your contribution to the whole. While you are at it, celebrate all the snowflakes in the iceberg and all the grains of sand. They too create the whole. In other words, give to the animal, the plant and each other as much respect as you give yourself. Treat the king as equal to the pauper. In physical body, each person plays out a role. In spirit, all is equal. Rejoice and celebrate all of life. Love fully without hesitation. Take a moment to feel the love within. Feel it for the entire whole. Breathe in to the love of all. That is an action to practice. Begin now.

THE FORMULA FOR HAVING ALL

Let's continue talking about love for all. Changes will have to be made. Perspectives will be altered. Beliefs will need to be challenged. This could be fun if you let yourself go. There is a purpose for letting go of old ideas and believes. To simplify, if you aren't having fun, peace, love, joy, then let go of beliefs which are in the way. Probably your beliefs are limiting. Limiting beliefs sound like, "I should have or I want... job, more money, smarts, home, or a lover." Let go. Embrace that which you have. Embrace spiritually so that it will materialize physically. What you have spiritually is a connection to infinite intelligence, love, abundance. Become one with infinite love. Feel the love in your spirit. Practice. Once you begin to feel your connection with infinite love, your thoughts and beliefs will change and you will become more peaceful. Once you are less needy and more peaceful, paths to physical love will open. That is the formula. You can have it all, start with the spirit, and then watch for the physical results.

RESURRECT RE-CREATE

We want to talk about resurrection. It is time to hear more truths. You see, resurrection is about rising above. Resurrection can be the rise of new physical conditions, the rise of spiritual enlightenment or the rise of a skyscraper. We want to talk about resurrecting awareness of your infinite self. Would it make a difference if you could understand that your life is infinite? Your spiritual life, the living part of you, will go on forever. In energy form, you will glow weightlessly forever. It is only your physical body that has a limit. Because you are in limited physical form, now would be a good time to make the best of it. The very best of now is evidenced by joy and happiness. That is why we keep repeating, and repeating- live in joy. This is your time to make the very best energy that you can offer to yourself and the world. We suggest that you throw a bit more caution to the wind, develop more trust in your infinite knowledge, and make a point of love and laughter. The stuff that you create a drama about can be reduced and therefore making space to resurrect joy. With the positive energy of joy, positive physical stuff will have an easier path to you. Re-erect joy. Re-create positive high frequency energy while you are in physical form. That is your job.

YOUR ENERGY BECOMES YOUR STUFF

Now is the time to consider that good things come from good energy. That is to say, the energy which channels through you becomes your physical stuff. Fine tune awareness of your energy, your feelings. Strive to become conscious of unconscious thoughts, beliefs, and feelings. Know thy self. Come to know the energy you emit. Become aware. Become conscious. The easiest way to alter your path in the physical world is through awareness of the energy which runs through you. Your energy is a result of the thoughts and beliefs that you act on. Therefore, when you talk about others, talk with kindness. The same goes for all of your actions towards yourself, others, and your environment. The energy you use is what you experience. Choose to experience high frequency, positive energy. That is your connection to the good stuff in the physical world.

We will give a few examples. If you are positive with the energy of money, positive physical money is what you will get. If you are positive with thoughts of friendships, positive physical friendships are what you will get. First, you create the energy from within. Second, the physical stuff will respond. This will happen. Become aware of unconscious, old ways of believing. Clean out the negative debris and make way for the good stuff.

THE POWER OF YOUR BELIEFS AND ACTIONS

We want to talk more about the fastest, most direct path to happiness. That path is through your beliefs. Let's talk about the differences and similarities between acting and believing. You see, the energy of a belief manifests into an action. The energy of an action manifests to move the energy of your world, your planet. The energy of your world, your planet moves energy for the universe. Everything works together. All energies affect other energies and all of life is made from positive energy. Imagine planet Earth glowing with positive energy for the universe. Those waves of invisible life forms which can travel through forever and will last forever are moved about by you-powerful you. We want you to understand the power of your beliefs which create an action. What we are telling you is that life on Earth is important. You are important because you can move energy. We are also saying that if you are happy then god, infinity, source, the whole is happy, and life continues. Yes of course we know that life will continue with or without you. We also know that each of you contribute to the energy of forever. Believe in yourself. Believe in your power. Believe that you are loved. Take an action on that belief... even a smile will do. With gratitude, we believe in you.

A REVIEW

We think it is time for a review. The best part of life is lived in positive high frequency energy or HEF. We are certain that you understand this by now. We hope you are beginning to realize that you are more than your situation in physical life. Your situations are both high frequency and low frequency. By that we mean both good stuff and bad stuff is a part of your physical experiences. We want you to know that you can create the good stuff by using high energy frequencies of love, joy, happiness, fun.... Believe in the power of goodness and love. Believe in gratitude. The greatest part of life starts with a thought and a belief. Start now for yourself, your community, your Earth. When in doubt, start with a good thought.

LEGACY

Moving on and forward, from this moment on, starting now, you can make a plan for contributing to world peace. It would be your personal plan, your legacy of your time on Earth. Your contribution can be simple such as more smiles or complicated such as resurrecting a conglomerate of togetherness in peace. Think about it. Begin somewhere- anywhere. Your legacy will live on long after you are gone. Your legacy will be the energy that moves through infinite time. Now that should put a grin on your face. More important than a grave marker or a statue of you is your infinite legacy. While you are in physical body, you have the ability to create HEF- high energy frequencies of movement. We smile at your ability; we are grateful for you.

IN APPRECIATION OF LOVE

We have much more to say regarding our love for you. Let you and us take a moment to feel appreciation. No matter your current circumstances, we want you to feel infinite love and our love for you. Allow it to radiate through you and surround you with a peaceful glow. Right now is a good time. Accept that you are love. Accept our gratitude for you. It is with great appreciation for you that we send our love to each and every one. As has been said, we don't stand in judgment of your actions while in physical form. We stand in love of your true self. Now is a good time to breathe in to the love surrounding you and running through you. Now is a good time to appreciate YOU. We do.

Now is another good time to appreciate all life forms. That would of course mean each other, all the animals, the plants, and the minerals. I think that includes all of Earth. Appreciate Earth. Know that Earth is alive and breathing just like you. Know that because of the living breathing Earth, all life is nourished, all plants can grow, and all animals too. Your planet is alive. Be grateful. Take the time to say thank you to the living energy of Earth. Appreciation and gratitude will go a long way. On an invisible level, the energy of earth will absorb your appreciation. It has to.

Now, walk in peace knowing of your greatness. The time has come for you to share your greatness with all of Earth. This is the dawning of a new age for your planet, the age of peace. You are the deliverer of peace. It is within your capacity to do so. Begin with dropping the dramas which hold fears- negative energy of hate, anger, pity, depression…. It is within your power to do so. Practice by becoming aware of your reaction to an action. Become aware of yourself. Of course you will always cycle through all energy frequencies. We are just saying that the time is now to spend more time in positive high frequency energies of joy, happiness, love, gratitude…. By doing so, you will experience higher levels of prosperity for yourself and for all others. It is a win-win game.

YOUR GIFT OF JOY

Good day. All is well. We are here to tell you that all is for the greater good. The time has come to celebrate. Life is immensely full of joy. If only you will focus your attention and open up to the "HEF" high energy frequencies as often as possible. Let it be known that life is for enjoying. It is your time in body to create high energy. The side effect will be that you too enjoy the creation. With each day we ask for some sort of joyful movement and joyful noise. Know that you will be living life to the fullest when you live joyfully. You see these words and you understand them. The next step is to create an action of Joy. Be the joy- for a moment, an hour, a day, a life time. Whatever you can do to contribute, now is the time. In time, this will get easier for everyone until it becomes a natural instinct. Low energy frequencies will become rarer in you and in your world. For no particular reason, take time to feel the joy within. Then act on it. Share it. Grin, smile, be silly. Find a good action for sending joyful energy from planet Earth into forever. Your infinite gift is joy.

We want you all to remember and focus on the outcome of behaviors. That is to say, if you remember your purpose of being in physical form is to move energy, then focus more on the outcome of your behaviors. What energy did you move? Was it positive, negative, or

neutral? Did you kill another, deliberately hurt another, or say negative words to another? Look at the reaction to your behavior. Look at
how it vibrated through others. Not just the victim, but to all those
who know the victim and to all those who know the knowers, and past
what you are able to see. The energy travels much further and affects
many more than you can see. IT IS AN ENERGY!

INVEST IN ENERGY

Today let's talk about NOW being the time for investments. It is usually a good time to invest in yourself, your country, and your world.
Of course, the investment we are talking about is resources. Energy
is your most valuable resource. The good news is that everything
is made from energy. The focus then is on the type of energy. As
you probably know by now, the most efficient, life sustaining energy
comes from high frequencies. You call it love, joy, happiness…. High
frequency is the energy of life- survival. Low frequency is the energy
of extinction.

   Imploding, exploding are continuous movements through all of
time. Now is the time for Earth to expand and grow- to explode positive energy into the atmosphere. This is where you become useful.
You see, you are important to the great plan. You are more than a
small life form in your current situation. We hope you will take the
time to invest in forever. The benefit is for you, your country, and
your planet. The payoff is, shall we say "out of this world." Invest now,
smile now, dance now, and celebrate something right now.

NEW BEGINNINGS OF PEACE AND PROSPERITY

Now is the time to consider new beginnings. Let's start with peace. A
new chapter, a new page is to be written in your own personal book
of peace. You are alive in physical form; therefore you have the ability
to begin your next page of peace. Start with words of love for yourself,
and then find words of kindness for others. Make it a habit to add
new words of peace each day. You are the beginning. You create the
gateway. As you spread words of peace instead of judgment, hate, etc.,

notice your responses. Notice how others respond to your peaceful message. The message can be as simple as one kind word. You won't need a stage or a microphone. You only need a word of peace for yourself or someone else.

This is also a new beginning of prosperity for all. You see, when you begin to feel prosperous, when you know beyond doubt, then prosperity will happen for you. Know that you are singled out just like everyone else to live a prosperous life. Begin the flow of prosperity for you and the world. Begin by believing. Now is the time to begin a peaceful, prosperous world. You hold the power of new beginnings.

We think you will want to know about the outcome of your existence on Earth in human physical form. The outcome is spellbinding. The outcome is a process of continued life with continued peace for generations to come. The next generations will create an abundance of peace. Their creations will sustain life on Earth. The beginning is now. The time is now for you to become aware of change. Become aware and alter the path. Allow the flow of life on your wonderful planet Earth. Do this by joining together as one positive energy planet. Join with your neighbors all across the world. Join in peace. Join in celebration of many life forms, all united on one planet with one source, whole, god, divine, energy connecting you all. It is done. Let it be.

INTELLIGENCE AND IGNORANCE

It is time to consider the pros and cons of ignorance. Consider that knowledge may be the key to survival. Consider that acting on knowledge may be necessary for survival. Understand that we are offering information to move life on planet Earth to a higher level of peace and prosperity for all. For everyone. This is the time to recognize and become aware of the movement into peace. You see, the level of intelligence on Earth is high enough to create life or death on Earth. It is too late to retreat into ignorance. A retreat into ignorance sounds easy and possibly satisfying but there is too much intelligence to allow ignorance to dominate. You see, the intelligence of a few has power both pro and con. A few intellectuals can increase life sustaining activity, or can create devastation. The results will be because of power, greed, fear or the desire for peace and oneness- a united planet. We want everyone to develop a connection to high energy frequencies. The connection is made by tuning into your connection to the whole, source, divine, god. That is your only choice. It is time to put your intelligence into the realm of forever. It is time. Everyone will play a part at this time of decision making.

PROSPERITY FOR ALL

Now is the time to consider a future of prosperity. Consider it. Really take action and imagine. Imagine all of the people on planet Earth being prosperous because new rules provided for everyone. Create in your mind a place where the weak and the strong have equal access to prosperity. It is possible. It can be done. Know that the time is now to pave a path that includes everyone. Those whom you may call unworthy are equal in worth. Stop the name calling and negative energy. Create a path which includes everyone. Only then will there be peace on Earth. Peace equates to joy and a thriving planet. Do you see how a mindset must change? The mindset of separation and judgment is in the way of peace. We want to hear words of love and acceptance of each other. Yes, yes it is very clear that some people are stronger, more educated, more beautiful, and more desirable than others. It is true that some people have weaknesses which are considered unacceptable or undesirable. It is time to drop that thinking. It is time to value every soul who has chosen to enter a physical body for the purpose of expanding positive energy. Every soul is playing out their role and walking their path in a current place in time. They are all needed or else they wouldn't be in physical form on Earth. Now is the time to praise each person and help them along their path. Help them along the path which may be different from yours. Help by praising instead of negatively judging. Now is an excellent time to begin greeting each other with infinite love. Greet with the highest power, which is freely available at all times.

It is time to crack the surface of negative thoughts and beliefs. It is now time to expand positive thoughts through awareness. Wake up people of Earth. Begin the prosperity for all. Do this by monitoring your own thoughts, beliefs, and actions. There is enough for everyone and everyone has a purpose. Everyone has the right to prosperity. The source, god, whole, divine energy provides for everyone. It is the human laws that allow some to prosper and some to be without. This is true in your religions, your medicines, and your politics. A hierarchy of separation has developed in all aspects of human existence on Earth. We think it is time to level the field so that everyone is valued and prosperous. Think about it. Visualize.

THE ACTION WHICH FOLLOWS YOUR THOUGHTS

What is your action plan? What will you be doing to make a difference? Have you thought about it? Have you begun talking to others about it? There are two good ways to begin. Think about it, and talk to others about it. A thought is an energy. An action is continuing along the energy circuit of thought. You do this constantly. Now we ask that you do this with awareness. Become aware of your thoughts and how they are on the energy circuit of your beliefs. To crack the crust, become aware. Awareness is a constant energy to monitor. Only through awareness will you begin to join the movement towards a peaceful earth. While your mind is being aware and challenging beliefs, allow your spirit to connect with infinite love. Once you are connected to infinite love, the work will be done for you, through you. Infinite love is positive. There is no negative energy, therefore no negative thoughts or beliefs are in infinite love. You can think of it as a resting place for all your concerns. It is a place to refuel with energy of life. Now, how is that for an easy path? We think you will come to enjoy the ease of positive thoughts and beliefs. We think you will enjoy having less stress, worries and concerns. We think the whole planet will be healthier and less stressful when you(s) become aware of your thoughts and beliefs, and when you consciously choose the positive. We aren't saying this to make you a good person. We are saying this to help you become a peaceful, joyful, less stressful person. Yet it is a choice. Your choice is your action which follows your thoughts.

THE ACTION OF VISON

Now is the time to consider a new direction which leads to peace. Do you understand that peace is an energy of Earth? It is available and can become a dominant energy source for all of Earth. Imagine it. Imagining is also an action. Imagination is something that you create. Create an image of peace. What does it look like to you? Stay with your image for a while. Let it grow until you believe it can be. Let it grow until you can believe in the possibility. We aren't asking you to move a mountain. We are asking you to imagine that the mountain can be moved. What we want you to do is see the possibilities that you create. Just see them.

In all fairness we will say that if you can imagine, see, and believe then the pieces will begin falling into place. The pieces, the energy of your desire will begin to manifest. When it does, watch for the changes. Notice and become aware of the changes in and around you. Start with just you, changing the energy of earth one person at a time. Don't bother trying to change everyone else at the same time that you change. Everyone else will be changing in their own time which may be before or after you. When YOU change, seek other like-minded changers of peaceful Earth. We can tell you that there are plenty. They live in abundance. Seek these changers. Connect with them. The peaceful vision that you created will explode with strength once you do. I think you call it exponential growth. We call it an energy explosion. Either way, hold your vision and connect with others who share the vision of peace for planet Earth. Watch the reality happen. Look for signs and indications. Look at the turbulence which is shaking up the beliefs in the world. Be grateful, not fearful. Know that the best is on its way. We admire your visions.

THE POINT IS, NOW IS YOUR TIME

We are getting to the point which is that the power, peace and existence of earth is within every life form. The point is that everyone can and will make a difference. What is the difference you want to make? Seriously, think about it for a moment knowing that you are making a difference. Is it the difference you would want it to be? At the end of your time in this incarnation, what would you want to hear people say about you? Oh yes, there will be talk. What would you want to say about you and your contribution to peace? Say it now. Say what you are contributing. Say it with a smile, a joyful moment, a hug. Say something about peace while you can- while you have a physical body and the energy to move with your words. Feel the infinite love within you. Know that this is YOUR time to spread your actions of peace. Your words, thoughts, beliefs, and actions are spreading through forever. Go ahead. While you can, fire up to your highest potential. Really! All that means is to have more fun, laugh more, feel love, and share it all with others. We think it is an easy assignment, even with all your dramas and struggles. Live in HEF, high energy frequency as often as possible. Planet Earth and far beyond depends on you. The point is you are alive now. Make the best of it.

THE FUTURE OF EARTH LIFE DEPENDS ON CHANGE

It is not a question. It is a statement that the future of Earth depends on change. That is to say that the future of life on Earth depends on change. As we have said, the planet can rebuild itself in time; a lot of time. But why go through killing off life just to start over again. The rivers are flowing. One is the stream of destruction; the other is a steam of life. Wake up. The choice belongs to each individual. Heed these words. Live in oneness for all or separate and destruct. This is your turn. This is your chance to create. We hope you will make purposeful choices which include all. We encourage you to believe in yourself and your power to create change. The personal direction of each person may be different, but each direction comes from the same source for the same goal. The source is love, god, infinite wisdom, the whole- any name you choose, the goal is expansion of positive energy. Each of you is connected to the same truth. This need not be an argument. Complete your path for this life cycle. Deliver positive energy. This isn't a question; it is a plan which was made before you entered physical life. It is your turn to act. Practice reconnecting to your inner truth. Your personal answers are there.

NOW IT IS TIME TO MOVE FORWARD

We are coming to the time of discovery. The people on Earth will discover a new way of being. Of course there will be resistance with some. Those with the largest amount of fear needing the greatest amount of physical control and physical comforts will resist the most. Let me assure you that love will conquer. Love from all will be stronger than fear from a few. The followers will learn to lead. The doubters will learn to believe. Watch the unfolding with awareness that it is meant to be. In the end, everyone will be living joyfully and in abundance. The only killings will be the necessary life exchange. You, the human, will exchange your life for those who devour your body just as other life forms will exchange their life form for yours. It is all in the cycle. Let it be. Begin living your life without fear for fear is your weakest position. You are a contributor to the positive energy of life. That is your purpose. Anything else is a waste of time. All other energies of negative impact are a waste. Judgment, drama, anger, fear, blame, jealousy- you know the ones. If you aren't living in infinite love for yourself and ALL others, then we suggest that you get back into balance. You can feel the disconnect or discord, and you can feel the joyful peace within. Don't settle for less than the best. The best for you is the best for all.

Now it is time to move forward. It is time to accept a change for peace. Accept the inevitable which means the past way of life is changing for the better. The future is exciting for Earth. At least it will be once the turmoil subsides. The ruckus and discord must run its course in order to bring awareness and a wakeup call to those whom will soon align with the greater good and greater truth of the whole. Let it be.

PRACTICE AWARENESS OF GREATNESS

And now, let's create a celebration. You see, celebrations and rejoicings raise the positive energy of you, all of Earth, and out into space. Make it a habit to celebrate. Don't deny the joy within. There is no need to be regularly solemn. Solemn is not the high frequency energy which you wish to obtain. Go forward with a heart of celebration. Meet each other with celebration. Of course that could be small as a smile or large as a dance. Express gratitude regularly. Express from your true self, from your inner self. Gratitude brings more joy because gratitude feeds into the energy of joy. What we are saying is to take note of the wonderfulness that you encounter each day. Be aware of greatness then be grateful. Practice.

EMOTIONS ARE YOUR ROAD MAP

Now we will talk about the comings and goings of your energy, the energy of emotion. As we said before, emotion is your road map which lets you know if you are on or off path. All positive emotion is on track. Keep it up. Notice, pay attention to what makes you happy and keep going there. Believe in your power of positive emotions. We are aware that "good and bad" things happen in the physical realm. Keep in mind that you exist in both the physical and spiritual realms. That is to say that you have both light and dense form. IT IS IMPOSSIBLE TO HAVE LIFE WITHOUT SPIRIT ENERGY. We hope you all understand. It is also impossible for all living things including plants, animals and yes, the rocks and dirt of Earth to survive without spirit energy, the energy of life. Your planet is alive. But this time we will call it your connection to the whole. Your planet must be connected or else it will cease to be. The positive life sustaining energy of infinite love equals life. Your emotions are your guides. Get on track and stay on track as often as you can. This is your opportunity while in physical form to create and move positive energy. This is your opportunity for your best life. Be your best as often as possible. Be positive, happy, and joyful, loving energy to yourself and to your world, as often as possible. Enjoy while you have the opportunity.

BEGIN NOW IN THE DIRECTION OF PEACE.
Now, we think it would be beneficial for you to know that the time
is now for movement in the direction of peace which is the direction
of positive energy. All of you as a planet can move into the direction
of peace and in time all of the people of Earth will move into peace.
Begin now. Open your mind to the idea of peace. That is an action.
That is a mental action to prepare you for the journey. Start the journey with thought, awareness, beliefs. Open up to possibilities. Open
up to the awareness that you can. Make it an "I" statement. You have
the power to create. Create love. Create joy. Create positive energy
frequencies. It is your choice, based on your beliefs. Let's imagine
that you don't believe in your power of peace. We suggest that you
act on peace even if you don't believe. Keep acting. Keep it up until
you see changes in your beliefs. When you recognize the changes you
will feel the difference. When you feel the peace within, the love and
joy within, it will radiate to others. When they feel your peace within,
they will connect from their peaceful place. And so it goes out into
forever. Yes, of course this will take time for all the people on the
planet to feel the peace. Start now. The revolution has begun. It is
time for you to join. Go forward with peace. Let it be.

UNDERSTANDING THE CONCEPT OF ONENESS
Let's write about this being the time for peace through oneness.
Understanding oneness means understanding one Earth, one life
form, one energy for all. We understand that you see each other as
separate individuals and separate from animals, plants, and minerals.
We see you in that way also- and more. From another view, we see how
you all are a part of the same system. If you followed a thread through
all of life on Earth, it would encompass all. The single thread of life
that goes through you goes through each other. You all come from
and return to the same source. Let's break it down for you. Let me say
that you are the same air, the same water and the same physical mass
as all of Earth. Each individual eats the same substance of life that
has been recycled through forever. Everyone does. You and everyone

else sprung from the same material that created your physical form. Everything did. If we were to shrink all of Earth into a single cell, there would be ONE life form. Now after enlarging that single cell, you would be able to see individual components of that one form. You would be able to see yourself as an individual. Just like the grains of sand together form one desert. You are a part of the life of Earth. You are not better than or worse than. You are one with life on Earth. We like the view from outer space. We don't see the individual properties of life on Earth; we see Earth- one life form radiating energy. In order to maintain one life form named Earth, the energy must be life supporting. It must contain life supporting positive energy- the more the better. If you shrink all of life down to the level of energy, you would see that the source for all is the same. Everyone is a source of love, god, the whole, infinite oneness.... It simply makes sense to treat each other and your planet with the idea of oneness- kindness towards all of who you are. And you are all of this Earth through your life connection. You are a living breathing appendage of the larger body of infinite energy from which Earth came. Earth is also an appendage of a larger energy. So is your neighbor, your pet, your plant, and your rock. All are an appendage of the same source. Does that make sense to you? Good, because if it does, and if you start treating each other as a part of yourself, then life will be easier. Easier is the goal- an easier, peaceful, happy life for all. Do you get this?

YOU ARE A SEGMENT OF A LIFE-SUSTAINING GOOD TIME
We think it should be comforting to know that you are one of the crowd. You are all here to celebrate this party of life. You are one part of this wonderful planet. You are one drop of water that makes the ocean. You are one ingredient in the loaf of bread. You- joined with all else becomes all of Earth. You are Earth. And you are infinite. You have the power by being a part of the oneness of all. Now begin to create from this power of oneness. You can stop feeling separate. As we said, separateness creates a feeling of smallness. Smallness is the source of sadness, depression, anger, greed, judgment.... Know that

you are much, much more. Come to live in your greatness. Living in your greatness you will be living in love, joy, abundance, and happiness. Take your time getting to your greatness. We understand that it might be a new thought forming into a new belief. Begin by seeing yourself as one-of instead of one-separate-from. The value in you is the same as the value in them. All of earth is here to produce joyful energy. You are a piece of earth and your job is to create positive energy which sustains life. Make it an "I" statement by saying, I am a part of earth and my job is to be happy. Let's get this good time going.

JOINING WITH OTHERS FROM THE LIGHT WITHIN

Next, we will discuss the pros of societies. It is known that life forms tend to huddle into groups. We agree that there is a good reason to join together. We suggest that you look for and join with others of similar interest. It is with combined strength that the largest explosions happen. Create your society. Create your group of believers in peace. Join together to celebrate peace. No judgments, no hatred, just a belief in peace. You don't have to protest. You just need to brighten the light within you by joining with the bright light of another and another, and another. Together you all will create a surviving, joyful, loving planet. Each glowing group will eventually join with other glowing groups across the continent. It starts with believing in yourself- believing in you light, your power within. Start now.

We suggest that you make the basis of your society from love. The physical differences within your society are not relevant to love, joy, or survival of a planet. We want you to know that your new society will be necessary for creating a peaceful movement on Earth. Brighten up!

VALUE OF THE JOB

Today, let's talk about the time to reveal. Now is the time to reveal a bigger truth- the truth of abundant living. All of you want it. It is available for all. So why do some have and some have not? The truth is that some want more than others. Some feel that the most important aspect of being a human is having more than others. Or having all they can. Others don't seem to be so bothered with having all they can. Still others don't know how to get enough. They feel like a victim of unfair abundance. Let's talk about everyone having their portion. As you know, some people are in the position of power which gives more abundance. Still others will never have the capacity to be in power. With this knowledge, it is up to the people on Earth to choose a plan of richness for everyone. The plan is to create a system that cares for each other. Create a system that circulates through all. Believe that abundance will come back to you when you let it circulate. We aren't saying that good workers must share with bad workers. We are saying to put into practice a plan where everyone contributes and everyone receives. It isn't difficult.

We suggest a more equitable distribution which is brought about by placing more equal value. Here is an idea. How much do you value a clean toilet when you are at a restaurant or shop? How much do you value a governor? If you value a clean toilet, then maybe you will contribute more to the salary of the cleaner. How much more do you value the governor- or the entertainer, or the CEO, or athlete, in comparison to yourself? We can tell you with most certainty that most people will take as much as you give them. We can tell you just as clearly that you can take another look at your values. We suggest that you put yourself in the circulation. No matter what your job, place a value on it, and then enjoy the valued work that you do.

We can tell you that you place the value. We can tell you that you will equalize the pay. You are in a position of power to equalize abundance. Begin thinking about it.

MORE ABOUT VALUE AND ABUNDANCE

Create the value you wish for. Pay the value you believe in. This is a lesson in confidence and believing in yourself. You are not a victim of lack. There is enough and you are not singled out by the energy of forever to do without. It is up to you to believe. I need to say that louder. BELIEVE in your power to create that which you desire. We see the poverty, the starvation, the homeless. You see it too. We also see that it isn't necessary. You can probably agree. It is up to you to create the change you want. One person at a time, one community, one nation will make a difference. You can plant the apple tree or you can buy the apple from the market- your choice. That is to question where do you place value? Who do you believe in most- yourself or another? We say, believe in yourself. Believe in your power. Believe in your personal abundance. Value yourself as we value you. We see that you are all worthwhile and contributing to the expansion of Earth. We would equalize the pay system. You see, we recognize value in those who take care of others. We notice the value in teaching love for each other. The value is continued life on Earth. We recognize the greed in many. We recognize the powers which can destroy Earth. Do you think it is time to value those who contribute the most to the future of Earth? Do you think it is time to place less value on those who take more and give less? Value those who believe in all of life on Earth. Devalue those who believe in limiting or separating life on Earth. Believe in prosperity for all. Now, make it an action.

THE SPRING OF CHANGE
Let's begin with the idea of spring time- a beginning of change, a beginning of changing seasons. That is what will be happening for the people on Earth- change. Now is the time. It can't be ignored. The question then becomes, which way will change happen? It is now time to consider the destiny of Earth. We sincerely suggest that it is peace. A sure way of obtaining peace is to join together in acceptance of each other and all of life. Actually, that is the only way- acceptance of all and of the differences. Let's be clear; you don't have to like everyone or everything, yet it is important to understand and accept differences. Understanding comes from within. Understanding is not about choosing one team over another. Understanding will be about agreeing to have peace. When we say peace, we mean peace for everyone. We are saying to accept every life on Earth. We are saying to create laws and plans that don't separate. The best way to do this

is to create an understanding that everyone is important, and everyone is valued. It is no longer me against-you. It has to be me-for-you. The belief has to come from the knowing that everyone is equal and valued.

In this spring of change, know that peace is possible for all of Earth. Let me repeat, peace is possible. It is a matter of changing attitudes. The opposite of finding peace in this changing time is finding destruction and death. Yes, it is the time. We say the time is now because your planet is emerging into a new energy. The new energy cannot see survival or destruction any more than the ocean can see if a person will swim or drown. The energy of change will not be sudden. It will be a process happening over several generations. Start now before the damage is too great. Let me make it very clear that you, each of you have the choice. The energy of change is here and you get to decide the direction. The power is within.

The spring of change is not about creating fear or panic. It is about creating love and joy for all. Don't take this as a doomsday. Take it as a wake-up day. Wake up to the idea that life is a product of love. Without the highest frequency energy of love, there cannot be life. Can you get the connection and importance of the energy which you create? We think more people are beginning to understand. We want you to experience the spring of a loving planet filled with joy and prosperity for all.

LIVING IN INFINITE LOVE

We will write again about love as you call it. We don't call it by a name but we know it as HEF- high energy frequency. The energy of forever is similar to but not the same as the energy of a romantic human experience. The physical aspect of human love has limits and imposed rules and conditions, which brings both joy and sadness, and all types of emotions and actions. The HEF, high energy frequency of love is pure. It doesn't judge or discriminate. It doesn't have a beginning or an end. It is always available to everyone at all times. We invite you to tune in and feel its power. Practice finding and experiencing the love within which is different from your loving connection to the physical world. It won't be found in your head. HEF love will be experienced in your heart. It's a feeling, an experience. A good time to practice is when the brain is quiet... early morning or late at night?

The reason we bring this to your awareness is that no harm can be done once people begin to understand infinite love. While experiencing infinite love, one cannot experience negative emotions or negative actions. While living from this place of love, a higher truth will come; a truth that takes away much of the blame and suffering. This new way of living will increase good health for life on planet Earth. Is this beginning to make sense? Finding and living from a place of infinite love will increase the quality of life on Earth. We want you to become familiar with the greatest life, the greatest love. You don't have to stay in the frequency of love. We ask that you tune in, and get to know the feeling. Practice the art of living in love.

YOU, TIME, AND INFINITE LOVE

Now, this is a good day to hear about the lessons of time in a loving world. This is exciting and we hope you will think so too. Time and infinite love go hand in hand. You could almost say they are the same- almost. That is because infinite love, that which you are made of, goes through all of time. There wouldn't be time without infinite love. God, high frequency energy, the whole of all, divine, is all infinite love which is what you are also. Now, your body is limited in time, but it is recycled from all that is and all that will be, which makes your body, in a way, timeless.

It is good that people caught on to the idea of recycling which means reusing a material. All is going to recycle eventually but reusing and remaking from the same material is faster and more efficient for your planet.

Your spirit lasts forever also. The spirit of ____ fill in your name has been around for a very long time under the guise of different names and places. Your spirit recycles through life forms whenever it is ready.

What we want you to know is that time is the keeper of all things. All things change forms. The answers to all things are in the knowledge of time. We think this information is helpful for restoring peace. Once you realize that there is nothing to fight over, peace will come. You and everything else are timeless love.

I hear you ask about low frequencies of anger, fear, sadness. Yes, you are also low energy. While in physical form all frequencies are available to you. The difference is that low frequencies have limits. They cannot travel through forever. Low frequencies cannot sustain infinite life. We could almost say that low frequency is a waste of time. But it isn't because infinite time is not susceptible to a waste of low energy.

Now, do you find it exciting to know that you are a part of infinite love and that you recycle through forever? Keep in mind that time as we see it is not linear. It has no beginning and no end. Therefore, you, time, and infinite love will always be. All the answers to always are within you- not in your physical short term brain, but within your infinite self. Practice tuning in to your larger you. We hear you ask how. We say, take time to get quiet. And there are always others in physical form who will help you. Seek and you shall know.

ENCOURAGING FACTS

Today we want to share with you words of encouragement and words that will encourage you to be your best self. We know that you all are aware of individual freedoms, or shall we say individual differences. Whether or not you are allowed to express differences is not the issue. The issue is that you have differences and individualities. It is encouraging for us to watch your differences swirl and change with your time on Earth. One year you are like one thing and another year you are like something else. We are getting to the point that change happens for everyone and everything. Because you know that change will happen, we suggest putting more focus on your changing self. For instance, there are times when you feel like dirt and then there are times when you feel so much better. Realize that as you go through these changes you can direct the path. You do not have to be a victim of your environment. It is encouraging to know that you are much more than your circumstances. Whatever is happening in your world does not define who you are. It is encouraging to know that you are, and always will be, more than your situation. With that in mind be ruled by your inner self, not by your environment. Once you start living this way, you'll notice that your environment begins to change along with you. You will be able to say. "Stuff just isn't as bad as it was." We hope this encourages you to be more fun- to lighten up on your reactions to stuff because you are bigger than and more than the stuff in your world.

WHEN TO ASK FOR AND GIVE ADVICE

We want to suggest that you take some time to enjoy Earth. Keep in mind that your stay here is relatively short in infinite time. Lighten up on the blame, jealousy, judgment stuff. We want you all to realize that everyone is going to do life their way. It may not be your destiny to change the path of others. A better idea would be to offer suggestions but do so infrequently, knowing that the situation and the people will change in their own time. We know that your good intentions are to help others change before problems arise. Sometimes it is the problem that will create the change, not your interference. Watch it all unfold, step in when asked and at all times be a loving witness to the journey of others. By the way, that is how we do it. We can see your problem, your negative energy of sadness or anger, and we love you anyway. If you ask, we will guide you. If you ignore our words, we let you continue.

To be sure, "you" are "them" just doing a different path. We see when you stumble, we see others wanting to help you, and we see when you refuse their help. We see you wanting to find your own way. We invite you to ask before the problems get big. Ask from your inner self, your heart. If you ask to have your loved one cured of a terminal disease, we may be able to do so, or we may be able to bring you peace with acceptance of the passing. We'll repeat a previous message—you were never meant to experience physical life alone. With that knowledge, we invite you to lighten up and shift into positive energy as often as possible. Do all you can to enjoy your time on Earth, knowing that someone is always willing to help you. We are here, standing by.

THE TIME OF FORGIVING
To forgive means to let go. It has nothing to do with a right or wrong behavior. Forgiving means accepting. It doesn't mean accepting a wrong doing but accepting that something happened and it is time to move on. This can best be done when you shift your energy from the perceived wrong back to yourself. Your energy is your responsibility. Your responsibility is to yourself, not to the wrong doings of someone/thing. We suggest that you move past that which you hold negative feelings about as quickly as possible. Grieve, move on. What we are saying is that YOU are suffering until you let go. Suffering is holding on to negative energy. Negative energy is of no value. Let it go. There. The sooner you rebound back to positive energy, the better you will be. You might want to plan a 'letting go' celebration, which means a forgiving celebration. Include all the positive energy you had about events before the wrong doing. Allow anger, sadness etc., to release. An example is, if your child was killed, remember, embrace, and celebrate all the wonderfulness of your child before it died. That would also mean a celebration of liberation and freedom from negative energy. Take an action to create the change. Forgiving is a part of the healing process. Make a choice to practice healing through forgiving. Reclaim your positive energy.

A REMINDER OF THE NEW PEACE ON EARTH
It is time to move on. There is a new world coming and you are a part of the movement. Your energy may represent delays in the movement, or fast forward ahead, or reluctance to move at all. Whatever your part, know that the movement is still here. We want you to know that Now Is The Time for a new beginning for Earth. A new phase in

development is with you. Prepare for the coming of peace. As we have said, this will take several generations. Some of you won't see it while you are in physical form, but will be seeing it from the spiritual side. We are pleased to announce again and again that the movement of peace is here. Just thought we would remind you. The turmoil that you may witness is a part of breaking down the barriers. The turmoil is enlightening those who need to see. Let it be. Rest easily in the knowing.

The message of peace is gaining momentum. Look up, look around, and see the messages of peace coming through. It isn't hard to see. It only takes awareness. Believe in the possibility and look for the results. Now is the time to look at signs of peace amongst the chaos, the ambivalence, and the resistant.

What you will see is joining together. You will see agreement and the desire to work together as one. You will see acceptance of differences. It is happening. Be assured. There will be great strides of coming together, as if streams are joining to form a river. Watch for the signs. Rejoice when you see. Rejoice with each other and share the word. Talk about the greatness.

THE FACT OF FEAR AND LOVE

Today we want to tell you about facting. We playfully created that word and it means fact checking. We will talk about re-creating your truth. From a new perspective it is time to redirect your energy of togetherness. It is time for everyone to assume a position of peace instead of a position of fear. We know that you don't always think of violence as coming from fear. So think about it. While there are a lot of assumptions that power is the answer to solving problems, having power to cause harm, create death, or to destroy is actually based in fear. You see, unconsciously there is fear that if you don't destroy, you will be destroyed, or shamed or.... Fearfulness is reprogrammed in a person's mind to look like strength and power. It's a way of fooling yourself. The best way to get at this is to know that fear is not and never will be power, no matter how it is disguised. If you are fearful, it looks like a negative emotion. It doesn't matter which negative emotion you portray it as. That means, spiritually speaking, if you are in a negative emotion you are in fear which is smallness. The answer is not to hurt another. The answer is and always will be love. Coming from a positive emotion will always deplete the negative emotion. Always. When you are spiritually strong, you are loving, tolerant, and coming from positive emotions. It can be no other way. When you love yourself you connect with infinite love. There is no fear with infinite self-love. There is nothing to prove, nothing to gain, and nothing to lose when you are connected to infinite self-love.

A COMMITMENT TO STICK WITH THE PLAN

Today we will talk about commitment- making a plan and sticking with it. Our plan is to have a peaceful planet Earth. We are the planners, you are the makers. When you join the plan and create the changes, Earth will be peaceful. Sound like a good plan? Good, then now is the time to begin. The ground work has been done; the seeds are ready for planting. The seeds of peace, togetherness, prosperity, joy, love—the world is aligned and in its proper place in the infinite system, solar system, universe, whatever you would like to call it. By any name, it is time for Earth to evolve in this system. Your planet is destined for much more. It can ONLY be achieved through peace and prosperity for all. Peace is the only path other than the path of destruction. LISTEN UP. The Time Is Now. The time of change is here and change is beginning. Choose. The choice isn't that difficult. Choose peace; choose prosperity for all. Choose to end greed which creates suffering. Choose to end war. Some other person's desire for power isn't worth you dying for. Choose to know that your infinite self will outlive the chaos on Earth. Choose to make your time here worthwhile. Wake up. Choose love over fear. Am I making myself clear? Love one another instead of hurting one another- at all times. Make a commitment to peace. Stick with the plan. We are here with you loving you through the transition.

THE HOW-TO OF FINDING THE LOVE WITHIN

Let's write about finding the love within. We hear some of you ask how. So we offer a how-to of finding the love within. It is done by feeling. It is a choice to feel love within. It is a choice to feel love without having an object to direct love towards. That means you can feel love. Simple and not arguably, infinite love is within everyone. Get quiet, practice feeling, notice your feelings and direct your feelings towards love. Bring awareness to your feelings. Notice. Believe in your infinite power of love. When other feelings arise, you have choices of keeping or releasing. Practice.

We want you all to know that everyone. EVERYONE has the ability to experience the love within. The love that is not associated with another person or life form- find it, allow it, get used to it. Become aware of your greatest resource- your power of love. Your source of life is love. Start spending more time there. Start with feeling the love within, loving yourself, then loving all else. The how-to is letting go of all else. Practice.

A TIME FOR JOINING ENERGY

We are ready to talk about a convergence of energy. The time is upon you for gathering your positive energies together and strengthening the flow. By joining together there will be an increase in productivity. That is to say that trickling water is powerful but not as powerful as raging waters or a flood. Join together and create a peaceful world. Join together and create equal-ness and oneness. Join together and create a movement of peace. It is happening. It is beginning. Deepen the momentum and let love for all, prosperity for all, joy for all reign. There no longer will be a separation of opportunity. In the end there will be agreement that all is equal. All of life has a purpose. All of life is here for the betterment of the whole. Let it be known that the field of power and prosperity will be leveled. Let it be known that by leveling the field, everyone will experience joy. Can you see how the current arrangements of power and powerlessness create negative energy? Power and powerlessness create greed, poverty, hate, prisons, and wars. Now is the time to focus on unity. Now is the time to start thinking about it. Start thinking about the kind of planet you will leave behind. What will your legacy be? Did you live to help with the continuation of Earth or did your life create destruction, famine, war in yourself, your family, your country, your planet? Everyone is creating and moving energy. Everyone has the chance to connect with others who are moving positive energy. Team up.

THE NEW DAWN HAS ARRIVED
Next, we are ready to share with you that this is the season of change. We have been talking to you about the change that is coming and about adjusting your beliefs. The time is now. Be aware of the changing tides of attitudes and opinions with people on Earth. Notice, look around and listen. Begin to believe and begin to act knowing that you have power. Each of you has the power to create the changes. You have infinite love and infinite truth to guide you. Trust in yourself. Believe in yourself before believing someone else. If your thoughts resonate with another's and the thoughts are positive, join together and strengthen. The movement of peace will be strong. There will be no denying the presents of the movement. The only denying will be with those who resist a movement of peace. Not everyone will be ready. As we said, this will take time. The movement will take generations before your planet lives in peace.

What a glorious day it will be when peace reigns on earth. It will happen. It is the destiny. The frequency of earth has aligned with the frequency of peace. Know that a new dawn is here. Rejoice in the knowing. And now, go forth and embrace peace. Be assured of the movement.

THE VIEW FROM A NEW DAWN
Now, we will talk about the view from a new dawn. The energy of the new dawn is multi colored, multi-feeling, with swirls of peace, rebellion, and chaos. That is to say the people of Earth will experience a wide range of emotions. There will be flares of anger mixed

with hand-holding peace. There will be resistance to the change and there will be acceptance. There will be confusion as past energy is released making space for the new energy of peace. We want you all to know that now is the time of change, and change is difficult for some people. Change is easy and welcomed in others. We say this so that everyone will have a better understanding of the situations. We say this so that people will understand and recognize the change without being fearful. It is not a time for fear; it is a time for transition. Accept the inevitable changes with knowledge that everyone will benefit in the end. The new Earth will be sustainable for all. Awareness of the inequality is being created now. The new dawn brings awareness with all of its conflicting energy. Step back and look at the view. Judgment is not necessary.

TIME FOR A REVIEW AND A REMINDER
Now let's review. You are hearing that each and every person is responsible for the creation of positive or negative energy on planet Earth. It is not necessary to look at others and judge them for the energy they create. By doing so, you too are creating negative energy through your judgment. A better plan is to find your truth within and live by it. This will take practice. Begin now because now is the time to change the energy of planet Earth. All is aligned and ready for your input. By working together in harmony, Earth will be prepared to extend love into an infinite cosmos. It is time for residents of Earth to think about meeting some of your neighbors on other planets. This is a good idea only if Earth is peaceful and loving. The idea of war and conquering other planets is old negative stuff. The new Earth will have long range, positive energy. Love- the infinite stuff that you are made of has the longest, purest frequency. Love is the energy that you will travel with. The time will come. Now is the time to practice the power of infinite love. Once again, we remind you to practice with others. Draw from the positive energy of others and give back from your endless supply. Reinforce and remind others as we reinforce and remind you.

KNOWING AND EXPRESSING THE LOVE WITHIN

The meaning of joy, the experience of love, the relationship with peace- this is what we have been talking about. This is what we wish for everyone on Earth. For some people the concepts may seem foreign and strange. It is true that some people have not known joy, love, and peace. For some, those experiences have been short lived and entwined with fear, anger, sadness. We want to share that there are many joyful, loving, peaceful people on earth who are willing to help you and share joy with you. For those of you with or without joy, love, peace, we suggest that you open your thoughts and beliefs for allowing and sharing. The easiest way to make this happen is to let go of fear. Let go of the fear of trusting, loving, and expressing. Be assured that you come from an endless source of love. It is your make-up. At your core, love is what you are. It is your loving core that we invite you to trust, and express. Love and trust from within so that you can love and trust another. That is what we want you to know. That is what we want you to practice.

CELEBRATION TIME

Now is the time to celebrate. NOW is always a good time to celebrate so we suggest that you don't put it off. Think of it like a child. I want it right now! Candy right now. Think of the candy as joy. For adults, the candy is a joyful celebration with gratitude right now. Add champagne any time you choose. The point is to celebrate with gladness at any time... and right now is a good time. When it comes to the good stuff, don't put it off. There will be more and more good stuff as you continue to celebrate. We are saying that there is rarely a need to delay gratification of something you want. As an act, be grateful and celebrate even before you get what you want. You can celebrate the thought of getting what you want. All of this celebrating with gratitude brings joy and the fulfillment of your desire. We suggest that you allow the child within you to rejoice often. Keep in mind that the more joy you have within, the more joy you will be sharing with the world. The more joy the world has, the more peaceful life will be for everyone. The more peaceful your life, and the life of Earth, the more positive energy you will be sending out into the forever. Now isn't that a good reason to celebrate?

THE BALANCE OF PEACE
Let's move forward with the idea of peace. For those of you in doubt, we say that it is doubt which is crippling you and keeping you away from peace. In this world, it is possible to live in peace or in not-peace. It is a choice. Our message is that the more people choose peace, the less non-peaceful experiences there will be on Earth. The energy of the whole will change. When the energy changes, so will the conditions. That means the more people shift into positive peaceful energy, the more pleasant the conditions of earth will be. Health, relationships, abundance etc., will shift when the energy shifts. More positive, less negative energy will equal more wellness, more abundance.

For those of you without doubt, who more often than not, enjoy a peaceful existence, we say that you are the evidence that peace can be experienced even in a world of turmoil. With that said, you are the example. We ask that you be an example for all. Live largely in your peaceful ways. Be the light of peace for others to see. Those in the shadows will benefit from your smiles, your acceptance, and your peaceful ways.

Now is the time to change the balance of peace in the world. You are here. It is your turn, your choice, your power. Now.

THE TIME OF CHANGE
It is time for opening the doors of the future. Open the doors and walk into a more peaceful existence. Imagine a world of radiance. That world is before you. Much of the suffering experienced in past generations will end. Imagine a life of abundance for everyone. It is time for this reality to be. The obstacle to be removed is mind set and we see many minds changing and opening. We are pleased to see the development of peace. We see this from our view yet we know that many people on Earth won't be seeing this view for a long time.

Some will not see it at all while in physical form. Yet the change is in progress. Awareness is being made. The pot is being stirred. There will be feelings of change across planet earth. From the rumbles will come celebration and joy followed by peace. Many of you already understand this. Over time the light will shine for all to see. That means awareness will be in everyone. Look kindly upon the children as they will be turning the tide. They will see more quickly the threads of love, joy, and peace that flow through us all. Watch for the miracles of acceptance for one another. Be aware of attitudes of change. Know that the time has come. Rejoice in the knowing.

Let's look at the turning tide, the shift in energy, the new beginnings, the glory days. Want to know what that means? It means that one person's pleasure doesn't come at another person's doom. One person's abundance doesn't come from other person's poverty. One person's freedom doesn't come from another person's slavery or confinement. Are you beginning to see the picture? Are you beginning to see that everyone will begin to enjoy life on Earth and no one's life will be at the expense of another? When mindset begins to change, so will peace for everyone. When judgments stop, so will separation and privilege. Look into the future. Look into the eyes of your neighbor. Begin to see kindness and equality for all. That is when the tide will turn, the energy will shift, and the glory days will begin. All things are possible.

A GOOD TIME FOR ALL

Now we want to tell you, this is the time for good fortune. Not for just you or you, but for all the 'yous' on Earth. Claim it. Stand up, stand out and claim your good fortune. You are fortunate to be living in a time of change. This is an earthly revolution and you are participating. You need not be afraid of the changes going on. Get out of your comfort zone and look beyond tomorrow. Look past the horizon, where you will see a new world coming. Shake off the dust of your existence, the dust of the past. There is a new day coming and the time is for everyone. You are no more or no less than your neighbor.

No better and no worse. Each of you is here for a reason and you all spring from the same pond, the pond of love. It is the infinite pond of forever more. We want you to understand past your limited brain. You see, you are a part of a big picture. The highest energy of love is what keeps the picture alive. Not love for just a particular person, but love for all. We would like to say that we don't call it love. We see it as the highest energy form, the brightest, longest reaching, and most powerful force of all. It is the force of life. Life springs from this energy force. *IT IS YOU*- and you and you and you- all of you. All of you are alive because of the energy of what you call love. We see it as the highest frequency. Our point is that, good or bad, better or worse, richer or poorer, you are all the same core make-up of infinite love. You all have different missions on Earth. Being a steering wheel or being a tire is irrelevant. You are all needed to drive the energy of positive love. You are all valued equally in the big picture. We don't see the separation that you experience. Well yes we do see it but we also see beyond. We see one planet struggling within itself. The struggle is almost over. It is now time to produce effortlessly in harmony. This will happen when everyone works together- peacefully. Do you get it? Do you see past the horizon? Can you imagine the good fortune for all of Earth? Everyone is a part of everyone. We think it is good that everyone has everyone.

GOODNESS IN EVERYONE

Today is a good day. Every day is a good day to reflect on goodness. We are ready to speak about the goodness in everyone. Every single person has goodness as a part of their makeup, their spiritual DNA. What you see in another is your choice. You may see the acts of kindness - unkindness, of love, hate, or good deeds and wrong doings. Our suggestion is not to focus so much on the bad acts. The person also has good acts. Find them, focus, and comment on the goodness that you see. If you can't see the good act, keep looking. It will show up. We are sure that everyone has goodness.

If you can't see the goodness, look at your own goodness and reflect on to others. Look at your beliefs and thoughts. Look at why others have different beliefs and thoughts. Look at the things that generate goodness. What we are saying is to sharpen your view, fine tune that which you look for. Once you do, you will begin to see more goodness and then you will act on more goodness. Once you start acting from a place of goodness you will feel better and so will the world. See how it works? Build momentum by starting with yourself. See the goodness within yourself then share it with the world. Practice a bit each day. Notice. Become aware of the goodness in you and in them.

FAST FORWARD TO THE AWAKENING

Now it is time to talk about the adventure- the road to health, wealth, peace, and joy. It is to be the experience of Earth to join others in the galaxies of infinite space. It is your time to become one with a greater space. You see, this can only happen with infinite love because infinite love is what space is made of. Doesn't that make sense to you? Doesn't it make sense that a high energy frequency is necessary to sustain all that is? The high energy frequency which you call love is also the essence of life. Love, god, source, divine, the whole... is the highest frequency which sustains life. It is time for earth to join in. And you will in time, one way or another. One thing we all have is infinite time. We suggest that you give up the battles and join the strongest force that exists. Give up your greedy, hateful, low energy, judgmental selves. What a waste of time. No problem though. If you want to use time in negative energy, it is available. Just look at a child throwing a tantrum. At some point it is time to stop the fit, get up, become aware, and get back to love. It is that time for earth. Wake up, get up, become aware of the bigger picture, and get back to love. This is a fast forward into the future. Your choice. You can sit in your negative energy for as long as you choose. Just know that the day will come when you wake up to us. Earth will wake up to love, god, positive energy, joy--so stay tuned to the awakening.

THE GOOD NEWS: ALIGNMENT WITH POSITIVE EXPANSION

A wonderful good day. That is the news we are bringing you. We are bringing you news of the development. We are pleased to present the evolving of earth. Yes, we know that you have already been told. We want to make sure you understand what this means. It means most of your suffering will end. The energy of earth will become mostly positive. Therefore healing will happen, disease and illnesses will be less, abundance will be shared by all, and relationships will flourish with the knowledge of infinite love. Don't you agree that is good news and something to celebrate? So go ahead begin the celebration. You see, an energy portal has opened and in alignment with positive expansion. Now is a time for rejoicing. Even though some of you will never experience the movement into positive energy, it is here. Now and for the next few generations this movement will be a positive force.

Yes, you may call this either a prediction or a truth. Some of you already believe that a change has come, while others will not understand. We want to be sure that you hear us. You all are carriers of the ball of positive energy. In time, you will recognize the shift away from negative energy. You will see more people joining together with common beliefs. You all have common beliefs because your commonality is at the core of everyone. The common part of every living force is pure infinite love. The more people move into this direction, the better life will be on earth for everyone. It will happen. Let it be.

REVOLUTIONS OF CHANGE

What do the light bulb, the automobile, the telephone, and infinite love have in common? Right, they are all revolutions of change. Just as those physical items changed life on Earth, so will the recognition of infinite love change life on Earth. It's revolutionary. All you need to do is dream, think, believe, and create. The process is the same whether you are inventing a gadget or inventing a society.

- Dream about that which you desire. Create an image. Visualize world peace. Can you see it in your dream state? Are you pleased with your vision?
- Think through some of the technical stuff of how to create the dream. What must YOU do to make it happen?
- Believe you can and that it is possible. Believe in yourself. You have the power and support of infinite sources.
- Create by going into action. Speak your truth. Be what you want the world to be. Then watch for the unfolding. Give thanks.

And that is the blueprint of change. Whether it is energy to power a city, or positive energy to power the planet, all revolutions of change start with a dream. It's your turn to dream big.

And now we can say that dreams come true. We are seeing the actions of many people which bring peace to Earth. Look around become one with all.

WEATHERING THE STORM

It is now time to talk about the weathering of the storm. During the change process, Earth will continue to look like a storm in the works. As negative and positive energy swirl around each other; the energy of earth will be of disruption. As you know, there is always calm after the storm. Choose the type of calm you would like to see. What will your grandchildren witness after the storm? What will all the GRAND children witness after the storm? Your choice, your creation. You can choose for everyone to get along and equally share abundance or you can choose the bombs, poverty, and devastation. There is only one way to win, and that is for everyone to win.

It is time to begin the walk through the storm. We suggest that you join forces with your dream of the future- whichever way you dream it to be. Keep in mind that the storm will also have bright light. Follow the light to peace. That is a metaphor for being nice, understanding, and compassionate, with diplomacy. We think you know what is meant. We'll be walking with you.

GO IN PEACE WITH YOUR ANGEL SELF

Today is a good day. Peace for everyone is on the way. Peace means that much of your stress and worry will disappear. Begin now. Begin to feel the peace within which is not associated with any of your earthly happenings. Pretend you are an angel. Pretend you are in spirit. Pretend you are weightless with love. That is what peace can feel like. The good news is that you are all those things and the feeling of peace is within you. Isn't that good to know? Now begin tapping into those feelings on a regular basis. Each day for as long as you can, imagine yourself being an angel in spirit form and weightless with the glow of love. The more often you practice, the more peace you will experience. The more peaceful you are, the less concerned you will be about the stuff out there. Negative stuff will still go on in your life, it just won't be as much or as important once you have the habit of being your angel self. That is what we mean when you hear the words "go in peace." Those words actually mean for you to tune into your angel, spiritual, loving self. "Go in peace" is more than just a way of saying good bye. Go in peace is a reminder that your loving spirit is with you at all times. Take advantage of it. If you are going to waste some time today, waste in peace. Of course it won't really be a waste of time. It will be a positive contribution to yourself and the world. Today is a good day for peace.

PAY ATTENTION TO THE ALL OF YOU

It is time for your attention to be directed towards progress. The type of progress we refer to is for the betterment of Earth. No single person can do this alone. It will take a shift of attention within everyone. Your world leaders will not be saving you or your planet. You, and you, and you will be doing this by paying attention- increasing awareness of the type of energy that you spend time with. Pay attention to your energy. Know how often during a day you emit positive energy.

Become aware of your kindness towards yourself and others. How often do you smile, embrace, or express joy? The more you are aware, the more your habit will grow. It won't take long before the effort is without thought. Your awareness will then be of the happiness and joy that you feel regularly. All the joy you have for no particular reason may come as a surprise to you. Much of your struggle will disappear and be replaced with peace. It's worth a try. We suggest that you make the attempts and see what happens.

Pretend that you have very little logical sense. Pretend that you aren't highly intelligent. Pretend that you are simply joyful for no good reason. That is a good place to start, because that is starting on your spiritual level. Once you master the art of living peacefully and happily, add it to your way of thinking and being in the world. Combine your love with your intellect. Start at the beginning. Your beginning is love. Pay attention to the signs. Create the path in all of your worldly adventures, beginning with love, joy, and happiness. Pay attention to all of who you are.

THE FLOW OF FOREVER

Let's talk about the comings and goings of space- the comings and goings of forever. You see, all of space is in constant motion. Like a breath coming in and a breath going out. All the energy of space is connected and must include earth. The connection is through the energy which you call god, divine, the source.... We think of it as the highest energy frequency for sustainable life. The whole, the source, is love. Breathing in rhythm is love. We would like to explain it differently but there are no words for this immense power, this magnitude of life force, this pulsating frequency of all that is.

We say 'all that is' because this force is a part of everything. This is bigger than imagination. You want to know where it comes from. It is self-generating and all of you are a part of the generation process. If you want to know where god comes from, study your life. Think of you as a metaphysical part of all. You are the answer to all. Not just the life of humans on Earth but of all that exists. God is love, is life, is a rock, a tree, an animal.... God creates and so do you. The god within and you creates continuity, a breathing and exhaling, coming and going energy. Is this beginning to make sense to you? We hope that you are beginning to understand your purpose. Your purpose is to create life which will equal love. One equals the other.

It all started as energy, the energy of life or the energy of death. You create. But you can never end forever. It's too vast for humans of earth to destroy.

YOUR LOVE FOREVER MORE

Next we will talk about the forever more and why you are a part of it. You see, without movement of positive energy on Earth life will cease. Not completely but unrecognizably. That is where you become a help. That is where YOU begin to radiate positive energy. Let me tell you that forever I have been saying the words of love. It is time to listen. How many ways can I continue to reword the same message, the message of love? It is more than your love for another person. It is an energy frequency of the purest kind. This LOVE frequency is necessary for life, and your planet is life. You are here on Earth in body to produce and spread the energy of love. This includes joy, happiness, laughter, smiles, and hugs. It is the glow in your heart that you feel. That is your purpose.

For those of you who say, "But I don't feel love inside of me," I say it is inside of you. Love is the stuff you are made of. It is impossible for you to be present without the energy of love which is god, source, or the whole of all that is. I understand that you don't always feel this love within. Or maybe an abundance of negative low frequency energy is consuming you. The negative energy was most likely put on you from another person with negative energy. It gets passed along. I am telling you to change the course. Heal yourself. Purge the negative energy from your wounded self so that love can be felt. You will know there is a wound if you are feeling sadness, anger, guilt, grief, or any other negative energy. Those negative feelings are not the real you. Love is the real you. Always was, always will be, forever more.

UNDERSTAND AND BE THE PEACE

We think many people are beginning to understand the message of love and the need for peace. We are pleased to see the transformations coming to life in many people. This movement is, in part, about survival of humankind on planet Earth. The only way to make this happen is to change direction in the stream. Change to the flow of positive energy. The change of energy will flow through endless time and space forever. The positive energy you create now will last forever. Your positive energy will feed and nurture all of life. Start now. We are asking you to feel the radiance of loving life. If you understand this in your brain, then good. Now transfer this knowledge to your core. Be the smile, the glow, the happiness, the joy, and the love from within. Dance, sing, be silly, and play. That is what we are asking of you. That is your purpose. Take this to heart. Become one with your true self. In joy, enjoy living in peace.

RIGHT NOW, IMAGINE PEACE

Welcome to a new dawning of your civilization. Exciting. The very best is right in front of you. The very best is peace for everyone. It has begun. It is with joy that we announce the coming of the new way of living.

Do you understand the idea of 'the meaning of peace for everyone'? Imagine. Earth has not known this experience but we think you can imagine it. We know that you can see portions of peace every day. Magnify the portion you see until you can hold the image of everyone on Earth having the experience of peace every day. If you can see it, in your mind, then it can become real. Peace on Earth will start with imagination. Next it will become a belief, and then a reality. The time to start is now.

We ask that you take action right now. For a few moments, imagine peace for all of Earth. It has to begin somewhere. Let it begin in your mind. It is time.

LET GO OF THE DRAMA, MOVE ON, CELEBRATE

Good day, a wonderful day to celebrate life on Earth. That would make it another Earth Day celebration. We say the more the better.

Celebration means a time of joy; therefore every day is a good time to celebrate and experience joy on Earth.

We want to remind you that the power is within. The power to create whatever you desire is a part of your make-up. We recognize that conditioning can be a big problem. Everyone has been conditioned to behave in this way or that way. We are asking that you reconsider your actions. Think again about where your beliefs came from, and why you respond to a situation in a negative way instead of a positive way. We hear, "But the pipe burst, the tire went flat, the pet drowned…" We see your situations, we hear your complaints. We want to hear more gratitude and joy. The world didn't stop with the pipe, the tire, or the pet. There is still time for more joy in your life because you are still a-love, alive and producing high frequency positive energy. Keep going. Re-condition yourself. Be conditioned with the expectation of high frequencies of joy, and happiness, through good times and undesired times. When the pipe burst and the tire goes flat, try laughing at the whole situation. Practice seeing the joy in what is and the fun of unexpected situations. When the pet becomes a part of your life, rejoice, when the pet leaves your life, rejoice for the love you had experienced. Give thanks for having a loving relationship. Let go quickly of the grieving, anger, etc., and move on. Make the most of your time on Earth. Make earth day as joyful, as often, as possible.

TIME TO PRACTICE AND RELEASE

Now it is time to reconsider- time to think again about the possibilities of entering the arena of infinite love.

A time of clarity is needed. We want you all to understand that the purpose of infinite love is to maintain the movement, the expansion of forever. We are doing our part to advise you so that you can do your part. You see, you do have a purpose, a reason to be here in physical form on planet Earth. Again we say that your purpose is the expansion of positive energy for all of earth and for infinite space. You are needed, you are loved, and there is gratitude for all.

It is now time to release your fears. Remember that your fears look like jealousy, fear of abandonment, of greed; fear of not having enough in an abundant world. Hate, anger- fear of letting go and accepting peace- depression, fear of separation from the whole. Whatever your fear, practice releasing. It is time to let go and practice knowing that there is a better way. There is infinite love available to you all, right now. Practice tapping in to the strongest, most clear, longest reaching energy available. Tap into the energy of love, peace, joy, and happiness. Strong enough to move mountains, change rivers, and reach into outer space. It is time. Begin now.

THE BEGINNING OF THE END

Now, we are pleased to begin writing about the beginning of the end, the end of negative energy on Earth. You see, there is a time of peaceful change. Many planets have transcended into peace. Earth will too. The change has begun. It may look like more upheaval and chaos on earth but this is necessary to bring forth awareness of separation. No more passive surrendering to negative ways of being. When politics separate within the office and within the country awareness is needed. When countries separate in civil war, when people separate by color, religion, or... awareness is needed.

Before the answers come, there will be awareness of the situations. That is still happening now as it has happened in the past. People of Earth see and feel disconnect. People of Earth will be looking at answers to peace. It has started. The movement will continue. Again, we suggest that those who 'see' and understand join with others who see and understand- that the answer is loving acceptance. Together your loving positive energy will spread more quickly. Know that loving energy is the strongest most sustainable and everlasting. Know the power of love will bring peace to earth. It will happen. Know this and let it be.

PEACE AND HEALTH

We will continue writing about the new peace which is coming. The absence of struggle is coming. It comes with acceptance of one earth, one love. Imagine looking through a telescope, seeing other stars, planets, and systems. Go to a planetarium to get the full affect. Imagine the white streaks of light coming off these planets. Imagine the light as energy. It is. Earth sends off energy also. When the energy is a flow of white light, other places in space will know that earth has found peace. And when Earth finds peace, there will be wellness and an end to diseases as you know them to be. Without disease and poverty, there will be peace. At any time you choose, healing can begin on earth. It is your choice.

We suggest that you think about where you are putting your thoughts, beliefs, and actions. If you are paying large sums of money towards health, you probably should pay large sums of love towards each other. Compassion, joy, laughter, love are the payoff of health for the people of Earth. In time, this will be understood. It is your choice as to how much time will go by before understanding the correlation between health and positive energy. Eventually, this will be understood. There is no other way. We say start now. Come together as one peaceful planet. Come together as a healthy planet.

AWAKEN TO THE PEACE WITHIN AND SHARE IT
This is the time of awakening to a new way of being on Earth. It is a peaceful, joyful time filled with much more laughter and happiness. You will see and experience this awakening as soon as you are ready. If you haven't already, start looking for signs. We tell you that the signs are everywhere. The peace will begin inside you. Don't focus on 'them' in the chaos and anger. Focus on you in the place of awareness.

Now let's get back to the joy of peaceful living. Joyful is the way life was meant to be. Yes, humankind got off track by competing with each other. The better path would have been working together for the good of the whole. The only way planet Earth will survive is by working together for the good of all the life on Earth. Your weapons of destruction are now too much, if used, for the survival of earth. If you want to maintain existence on earth, now is the time for peace making.

Now is the time for everyone to join in unity for the prosperity of one earth. No single person or group owns or dominates this planet. Every person and group will transition out of physical form, or as you say, die. The most important thing a person can do while in physical body is live joyfully and peacefully with others.

The easiest, fastest way of developing a peaceful planet is by starting with you. Find your personal peace within. Make a conscious effort of working at it until you find peace. Then share from your peaceful place. Find joy within, then share from your joyful place, find respect within and share from a place of respect. Find abundance within…. you get the idea. Always start with yourself, then share, act, react, and be from that place within. The survival of earth depends on your personal awakening. Begin now.

COMING TO AGREEEMENT THAT LOVE EQUALS LIFE

We- you in physical and us in spirit are coming together with agreement. We feel that you are beginning to understand a greater purpose for physical life. It is becoming clear that we are one energy and that love equals life. It is becoming clear that you are in physical form to move positive energy. We in spirit are guiding you. It is our job to help you with your job. Believe in us as we believe in you. Together we will create a peaceful, life sustaining planet.

We are not your inner connection to the whole; we are not your connection to god, source, etc. Just as a parent is a loving guide for the baby, so are we a loving guide to you. Now, together let's create peace on Earth. We will not guide you to "blow them away." We will not guide you into killing fields. If that is where you go, then it is the choice of your brain and not the choice of your connection to infinite loving life. Take time to listen inside. Make a decision based on the truth from your heart (your connection). Your planet is chosen to survive and thrive. It is your turn, but only if you choose it to be. Let us know. We are standing by.

The time has come for answers regarding the future of earth. Yes we know. Earth will survive with or without humans. Will humans survive with or without planet Earth? Your choice. We can tell you, peace, appreciation, love, acceptance, joyfulness, and equality is the answer. The bomb is a metaphor of the brain trying to show dominance. It will never win. But maybe it will kill the planet. The greatest power is love. Love will win. The final truth is the highest energy frequency of love. Infinite love cannot be destroyed. Do you get this? Are your ready to face the facts? Give up your hard core beliefs. Know that you are amongst the greatest power available. The power of love is the power of life. Can we agree on this?

YOUR NEW NORMAL

All is well. All is as it should be, evolving as it should. You are a part of an evolving forever. You participate in an ever evolving, ever swirling energy. As a participant you add to the swirl. You stir the pot with the energy you put into it. We want to suggest that you add a little sugar and spice from time to time. That means to add kindness, joyfulness, and love, along with funny, silliness, and adventure. After all, you are a creator while in physical form. You are the creator of the energy which you stir. You are the vision of the future. We want you to know the time has come to create that which you desire, and not which you reject. Be what you desire, not what you reject. The swirl of energy which you create will swirl through and around you before moving out from you. Create your own joy, happiness and self-love not because we say to but because you want to. Create not as an outcome of what others or saying or doing. Create regardless of the others or of the experiences coming to you. Create from the core of who you are for no other reason than- you can. Start now. Eventually, this type of creating will become your new norm, your new normal way of being. Then you will be living in the peace that you created for yourself. Experiences will still happen but you won't be sucked into the drama. Experiences will come and go with peace remaining inside of you. This takes practice. Continue to read about, talk about, and experience your peace within. Eventually, you will know no other way. Eventually the world will know no other way. Keep practicing. Practice until you have created the new normal.

THE TIME IS NOW TO USE ALL THAT IS AVAILABE TO YOU

This is the time of change, growth, and the time of progress. The planet has entered into a new era. The strength of life on earth will greatly expand. The strength of growth is due to experiences, knowledge (brain), and the ability to connect with infinite knowledge. All three are necessary to bring about change. It is reasonable to think that one affects the others. That is to say, what good would be an experience without learning? What good would be learning without understanding the limits of the brain or the unlimited nature of infinite knowledge? You are here. The time is now to use all that is available to you. The time is now to go beyond limited behavior, thought, and experiences. Once you begin tapping into infinite knowledge, there will come the realization that smallness doesn't exist. Smallness is a part of jealousy, anger, starvation, greed, war. It is all an act of smallness, with a need for more. Once a person realizes the connection to the whole of all that is, negative energy will diminish as well as the drama built up around circumstances.

Let's consider the brighter side. Consider that once you connect to infinite knowledge or, call it that place in your heart or, the wisdom within, abundance will simply become a part of your existence. Simple. Your cup will runneth over with plenty. It is hard to imagine for some of you. Best we can say is to stop thinking about wanting and needing. Start living more often from the infinite love within. How would you call it? What words would you use to describe your connection to god, spirit, love, wisdom, the whole, the source? Would you call it a warm fuzzy feeling, an intuition, an -I just know-, a voice within, a reassurance from within, joy? We call it a connection. We say that it is a part of everyone and always has been. We suggest getting used to it and using it. The connection is here to serve. It is an energy. It knows how to keep sending when you recognize, acknowledge, grin and say thanks. In other words when you send a matching energy back, it knows to continue sending. Does that make sense to you? We hope so. If you haven't connected with this spirit within place, the time is now. If you don't know how, spend some time learning and practicing. It is time for you and the world to progress by using all that is available.

A NEW WAY OF BEING

Now we will write about discovery- realization and discovery of the new world. Well, not a new world but a new way of being in the world and a new way for the Earth to be. It is exciting to know that you have time and opportunity for creating this new planet Earth. It is our pleasure to assure you all that peace will come and that people of Earth will experience a new way of being. Be joyful with your celebrations of Peace Day. Begin to think of joy. Begin to look for joy and happiness. Stop looking at bad news. Stop reading negative stuff. Don't feed that which you don't want.

Begin to feed the energy of kindness. Take a closer look at what you bring into your life and what YOU PUT OUT. Become aware. The change will be with you. There is no other way. Awareness starts when you are ready. We are ready to see the changes on Earth. We are ready to lead you into a peaceful revolution. We are ready for your new realization and discovery of a peaceful existence on Earth. Other planets have this. It is your turn. Spend some time in awareness and imagine your best life. Bring it forward.

WE APPLAUD YOUR PEACEMAKING

It is all good. That is to say that the end result will show the progress of goodness. We are so very pleased to announce that the answers to your prayers for peace will be activated. That is to say, for all who have envisioned and supported the idea of peace, be assured that it will happen. You are creating the destiny and the longevity of your planet. The advancement will continue until everyone participates. For now, the leaders of the movement are paving the path. Resistance will happen because of greed and personal agendas but not forever. The time will come when everyone will see that what is good for one is good for the other.

We are pleased with the new energy evolving around planet Earth. In time, Earth will be a beacon of light for other planets to follow. The time is now to create the light. It is with much gratitude that we applaud you who are leading the transition into peace. We applaud the children of the next generations who will be carrying the realization of peace. We applaud that in future generations the people will be unaware of the struggles the past generations endured. We are pleased. The time has come. The time is now. Rejoice in the peace making on planet Earth.

IT'S YOUR TURN

Now is the time to enter a new way of being. Earth is ready. The people will deliver. We, the guides, will lead you. Your purpose is to pay attention so that you can actively choose the direction of peace. Awareness is necessary. Now is the time to move the energy of Earth.

The movement is towards the strongest power available. The movement is towards the power of love and its positive energy of life. Let's create. You are needed because you are in physical form which gives you the ability to create. You can do the kindness, the smiles, the hugs, and the acceptance. Those are the things which create positive energy for maintaining and sustaining life on Earth. Begin creating. Create randomly. Create with everyone.

POSSIBILITIES OF LIFE ON EARTH

Now it is time to consider the possibilities. There are endless possibilities of peace offerings. How many ways can you think of? Every day is an opportunity to offer your light within, your love within, your peace within. If only for seconds or minutes, so practice radiating through your peace. By doing so, you are healed within. Now help others heal within. Be the glow whenever you can. Tune in whenever you can. Stay as long as you can. Be the love, joy, and peace within.

This is an action plan. The action has to begin and now is a perfect time. Join with others in moments of glory. Reach out to others and draw them into joyful moments. Come together in peace. It is time to get this ball rolling. Time to end war, starvation, greed, judgments…. There is only one way to do this. The one way is through loving one another. The new norm will be kindness, appreciation, understanding, acceptance…. YOU are the beginning. You will start with challenging your beliefs. The movement will continue once YOU begin to lead the way. Be a strong leader. Open your hearts to the conviction that love is the strongest power. Love = life. We want to see planet Earth and its occupants alive and well. It's your turn.

TIME TO MAKE A DECISION REGARDING YOUR CONTRIBUTION

It is time now to consider the effects of war. The war or peace in your home, your neighborhood, your country is all contributing to the survival or destruction of Earth. It is time to make a decision about anger, retaliation, revenge, greed, and all the other stuff that people fight over. When we say "make a decision" we mean to think and look at consequences before reacting. The energy put out to destroy or cause harm will be the energy the planet consumes. The energy from negative behavior will also cause illness and disease. We tell you that the cure for disease will be available when positive energy consumes earth. You would be better off to stop paying to find cures, and start paying for positive energy. The good news is that positive energy is freely available to all. It is a choice, a decision, a survival. Somewhere, sometime, people will have to make the decisions for the survival of earth. The decisions will eventually be made by everyone. We tell you that the time is now. There comes a point when decisions are no longer available. Now is the time to turn the path into a loving prosperous planet. It is your turn earth. Which way will you personally go; towards or against the continuation of life on earth? Is the energy you put out into the hemisphere breeding life or death?

Take some time to ponder and evaluate your own contributions. In the end, the result will be because of everyone's contribution. The final killer will get his energy from the whole or, the continuation of earth will get its energy from the whole. There is no blame here. There is only an energy of love and life or an energy or devastation.

THE AVAILABILITY OF POSSIBILITIES

We are ready now to talk about possibilities as either limited or available. We are very certain that limits have no place in the whole of all, the love, the source, the god. Limits are only in the physical world therefore, your bodily behaviors have limits but your thoughts and beliefs do not. The reason we say this is so that you recognize the differences. It is our wish that you work with and tune into the unlimited thoughts and believes. We ask that you become more aware of your imposed "limited beliefs" and your restrictions. You see, it is better to think of possibilities then to think of restrictions. Become aware. Know that if you think it and believe it, the impossible can become possible. The idea is that a thought wave is energy which you manipulate. The same is true for a belief- merely an energy which you manipulate. It is time to practice manipulating energy for the goodness of all. You can start letting go of those limiting thoughts and beliefs, those beliefs which are restricting behavior. We know that most of you are "trained" by your beliefs to have restricted possibilities of behavior. We hear your denials. We hear you say, "But I can't, I won't, I don't want to." We say you are setting limits which you imagine to be real. It would be much better to remove the limited thinking and open up to the possibilities of the greatest, most joyful life that you can create. If you are living joyfully, you are probably living with unlimited thoughts and beliefs. If you are living within limited beliefs, you are probably suffering and creating suffering for the entire planet. Challenge your beliefs, your thoughts, and look for the possibilities. Allow opportunity to open. Watch for it in all the small or large ways and be grateful.

The key to abundance is to do your part with thoughts and be-liefs. Opportunities will then begin to present themselves.

JOIN THE MOVEMENT

It is time to discuss the coming of a new way of being. The time has come and the movement is on. Gather everyone. Gather in the com-ing of greatness. This is an invitation to step in to positive energy. It is a choice of action to take. We are not saying to read these words and dismiss them. We are saying for you to actively take a position of love, joy, happiness etc. We are saying to let go of your fear, anger, sadness etc. Create a reality of peaceful earth by creating the reality within you. Join with others in this reality of positive energy to increase the magnitude of strength. You have the power. You in physical form can move the mountain of infinite love. Move it, stir it up, and release the magnitude. That is your job. Now is your time.

Go for the truth. Go for the gusto. Enjoy the movement. The time has come for a movement into peace. The time is now.

ADDING TO THE MOVEMENT OF CHANGE

Now we want you to know that the time has come to move forward. Think of it as a major change on Earth. Think of it as how the in-vention of the telescope, the telephone, the automobile, or the light bulb, created a change on Earth. Know that in the beginning there will be doubt and disbelief. Know that, in the beginning, not every-one will understand. Know that in the end, everyone will embrace the change. Everyone will accept a peaceful way of living. In the end, a few generations away, everyone will live joyfully. Know for now that you are creating a new way of being for humankind. Your efforts will be for the sustainability of life. Know that the rumbles of change are here. The time has come to move the mountain of infinite love, peace, and joy. The move is towards the expansion of positive energy. Let it be. Allow this movement. Every smile, every laughter, every joy in your heart is adding to and allowing the movement. Keep it up. Keep up the good work.

WATCH FOR THE CRUMBLING AND WATCH FOR THE REALIGNING

Be aware; look for the signs of coming together. The time has come to live in prosperity. Everyone prospers and everyone will be happy because there is enough of everything for everyone. There is no need for hunger in a world of plenty. There is, however, a need for cooperation. This is what will be changing. People will be changing and cooperating with each other. The movement is on to bring about this change.

What we are saying is that there is a turn in the road. The river is flowing in a new direction. The energy of earth is changing. People will change also. Be aware. Watch, look, listen for the changes, and then join in. Notice the breakdown of old thoughts and patterns in your society, your country. Notice the breakdown of the ideas of separation. Us versus them will begin to shatter. In its place will be the idea of one Earth, one energy for all the people. This is what we are saying. Rules of separation will begin to crumble. Religions separate. There will be a crumble in religious separation. Wealth separates. There will be an equalization of wealth. Status separates. There will be agreement that all life form is valued for the position it fills. No one is more or less that another. Watch for it. Watch for the crumbling and watch for the realigning. Participate.

THE TIME IS NOW. LOVE IS THE WAY

It is now time to say that you have the messages of this book. Study them. Learn them. Practice living the truth of love. NOW IS THE TIME to begin living in peace. NOW IS THE TIME to break with old habits and beliefs. NOW IS THE TIME to know that YOU, at your core, are the essence of life and love and you are loved. We hope you will believe in us, your teachers- if not in us, then believe in the messages of love and sustainability. In the end there is only one way. Now you know the one way. The one way is love.

WITH INFINITE LOVE, WE GIVE YOU THESE WORDS

9 780998 178417